brilliant

budgets and forecasts

brilliant

budgets and forecasts

Your practical guide to preparing
and presenting financial information

Malcolm Secrett

PEARSON

Harlow, England • London • New York • Boston • San Francisco • Toronto • Sydney • Singapore • Hong Kong
Tokyo • Seoul • Taipei • New Delhi • Cape Town • Madrid • Mexico City • Amsterdam • Munich • Paris • Milan

PEARSON EDUCATION LIMITED

Edinburgh Gate
Harlow CM20 2JE
Tel: +44 (0)1279 623623
Fax: +44 (0)1279 431059
Website: www.pearsoned.co.uk

Originally published as *Mastering Spreadsheets, Budgets and Forecasts* in 1993.
This edition published in Great Britain in 2010.

© Malcolm Secrett 2010

The right of Malcolm Secrett to be identified as author of this work has been asserted
by him in accordance with the Copyright, Designs and Patents Act 1988.

ISBN: 978-0-273-73091-0

British Library Cataloguing-in-Publication Data
A catalogue record for this book is available from the British Library

Library of Congress Cataloging-in-Publication Data
A catalog record for this book is available from the Library of Congress

10 9 8 7 6 5 4 3 2 1
14 13 12 11 10

Typeset in 10/14 Plantin by 30
Printed and bound in Great Britain by Henry Ling Ltd, at the Dorset Press,
Dorchester, Dorset.

The Publisher's policy is to use paper manufactured from sustainable forests.

Contents

About the author   ix
Foreword   xi
Introduction   xiii

part 1 Budgeting and forecasting essentials   1

1 Understanding budgets and forecasts   3
   Definitions of budgets and budget forecasts   5
   Profit and loss forecasts   8
   Cash flow forecasts   8
   Spreadsheet-based budgets and forecasts for day-to-day
     management   12
   Forecasts – not the sole province of accountants   13
   Planning cycles   15
   Fixed, rolling and perpetual forecasts   18
   Can a forecast ever be right? Does it need to be?   20
   Summary   22

2 Using budgets and forecasts   23
   Budget management   25
   Planning and 'what if'   26
   Cost control   27
   Raising finance   28
   Cash flow control   30
   Summary   31

part 2 Spreadsheet essentials   33

3 Understanding computer spreadsheets   35
   How to use the example files   37
   What are spreadsheets?   38
   Examples of principal facilities and functions   40

Handy tips and shortcuts   58

Summary   61

4   Spreadsheet techniques for budgeting and forecasting   63

So many ways and means   65

Essential practices and conventions   65

Example forecasts   72

Examples of non-essential but useful techniques   89

Summary   94

part 3   Building the illustration framework   95

5   Preparations for the illustration budget   97

Are everyone's objectives the same?   99

Budgeting methods   100

Review of a budgeting process   104

The example business 'Widget Makers Ltd'   105

Deciding the requirements of the example budget   106

A single or departmental budget?   107

Cost categories   108

Cost headings   114

Categorising cost headings   118

Revenue headings   120

The forecast's duration and periods   121

Summary   122

6   Creating the illustration framework   123

The sales forecast   125

The budget forecast   127

The cash flow forecast   131

Summary   141

part 4   Using the illustration framework   143

7   Assembling the budget   145

Making the sales forecast   147

Making the budget forecast   150

Cash flow forecast adjustments   158

Charts and key indicators   160

Key ratios   165

Summary   167

8   Causes and effects   169
    Adjustment and refinement   171
    The reiteration process   172
    Examining causes and effects   173
    Simple cause and effect   173
    Address the cause or the effect?   180
    Gross profitability of each product   199
    Summary   202

9   Allocation, monitoring and reviewing   203
    Visibility, clarity and relevance   205
    Budget allocation   209
    Performance monitoring principles   210
    Setting up monitoring for the Widget Makers Ltd forecast   217
    Recording actual figures   224
    Reviewing the forecast   226
    Summary   237

10 Further analysis   239
    The impact of change on cash flow   241
    The effect of rapid growth on cash flow   248
    'What if' analysis   249
    Summary   250

part 5 Handling VAT   251

11 VAT in the forecast   253
    What is VAT?   255
    Calculating and paying VAT   256
    Cash flow forecast VAT calculations   261
    Summary   265

part 6 Measuring and controlling costs   267

12 Measuring and controlling costs   269
    First things first   271
    Absolute figures and percentages   272
    Measuring production costs   274
    Measuring manpower costs   275
    Activity based costing (ABC)   281
    Summary   284

part 7 A practical forecasting framework   285

    13 A practical forecasting framework   287
        Features and uses of the practical template   289
        Structure of the practical template   290
        Sales and direct costs   290
        Profit and loss/budget   291
        Cash forecast   295
        Asset register   295
        A typical month end routine   297
        Summary   301

        Glossary   303
        Index   305

About the author

MALCOLM SECRETT began his professional career with BT, initially as an Electronics and Telecommunications Engineer and then in a variety of management roles. After leaving BT he established a consultancy providing financial planning and forecasting, cost and productivity analysis and improvement, analysis of work flow procedures, quality systems, and the implementation of IT systems for financial planning and control.

Building on an innate ability to demystify and explain, Malcolm has developed a uniquely pragmatic approach to aspects of management all too often regarded as the sole domain of specialists – including financial forecasting and control, conventional and activity based costing, and the day-to-day application of spreadsheets.

His articles and books have been published throughout the world in English, Spanish, Arabic, Portuguese, Chinese, Russian, Ukrainian and several other languages.

Malcolm is the managing director of iBase Media Services Ltd, (**www.ibase.com**) a software development company specialising in digital asset management and digital multi-media library systems. He also offers business consultancy with special emphasis on increasing profitability through cost management, and the avoidance of insolvency.

Foreword

What this book will do for you

Whether you are a manager in the private or public sector, or a business-man running your own enterprise, this book will lead you step by step, using everyday English, through the principles of setting and managing budgets, and creating profit and loss and cash flow forecasts. You will see how to construct them on a spreadsheet, using examples and templates that you can download for free from the publisher's website.

Most importantly, having established an understanding of the principles of creating and managing forecasts, the book goes on to describe thoroughly practical approaches to business management using spreadsheet models that can be adapted to your requirements for day-to-day use.

Whether or not you have ever before prepared a budget, a P&L forecast or a cash flow forecast, you will soon be able to build and use budgets and forecasts that precisely match your needs.

Now – budgets and forecasts are, by their nature, very dynamic in the literal sense of the word, something never truer than when they are prepared using a spreadsheet. Books on the other hand are not, by their nature, dynamic in this literal sense – and there is a great danger that through them one of the most important and interesting tools available to managers is perceived as a dry and dusty subject.

So, our aim is to give you a grasp of the subject without sending you to sleep – despite your best intentions! And, equally importantly, to do so in a way that clearly shows what practical and dynamic day-to-day management tools budgets and forecasts can be when spreadsheets are applied to the task.

I've addressed these needs in three ways:

- *Firstly* – and most importantly – by making the example spreadsheet models used in the book available as downloads from the publisher's website. The idea here is partly to provide an opportunity for obtaining hands-on experience using spreadsheets for budgeting, and partly as additional emphasis to aid and accelerate understanding.
- *Secondly* – by using straightforward and relevant examples and illustrations from settings familiar to any manager or business person.
- *Thirdly* – by eliminating accountancy and computer jargon wherever possible. Where the use of technical terms is unavoidable they are explained, usually when they first occur.

Budgets and forecasts are viewed by managers and business people in many different ways, for example:

- for allocating and controlling expenditure
- for forecasting and monitoring sales volumes and revenue
- for departmental breakdown of the whole company's budget
- for supporting information for a business plan
- as the basis of a bid for raising finance or obtaining higher level authority for a revised strategy
- for profit and loss forecasting
- for cash flow forecasting.

There is no 'right' or 'wrong' use of budgets and forecasts. Although the list probably covers their most common uses, in reality there are as many applications as there are managers.

If you have previously prepared budgets on paper, you will certainly appreciate the enormous advantages of using a spreadsheet, and quickly see how much more you can do with them. And all of those things you had wished were either possible or practicable, you will now find are easy.

Finally, I hope you will find the book interesting, beneficial and most of all – enjoyable.

Malcolm Secrett

Introduction

The structure of the book

There are seven main parts:

- Part 1 – Budgeting and forecasting essentials
- Part 2 – Spreadsheet essentials
- Part 3 – Building the illustration framework
- Part 4 – Using the illustration framework
- Part 5 – Handling VAT
- Part 6 – Measuring and controlling costs
- Part 7 – A practical forecasting framework

The book can be read from start to finish, as a complete programme; or individual parts can be selected and read, or dipped into by way of reference. The contents provides a quick list of topics to help you find the section required; for a more detailed search, use the index.

Reference to computer spreadsheets

Because of the dynamic nature of budgets and forecasts applied to spreadsheets, and because spreadsheets themselves are inherently so versatile and dynamic in their own right, by far the best way to understand and appreciate the interaction between all of the elements is to use them in practice – to try things out for yourself. In this way you will soon become adept and this book and accompanying spreadsheets have been designed with this specifically in mind.

You can construct the spreadsheet examples for yourself, but it will be easier and quicker to download and use copies of the examples from the website.

Obtaining the examples

The examples can be obtained free of charge from the publisher's website at **www.pearson-books.com/budgets**

PART 1

Budgeting and forecasting essentials

This first part of the book looks at budgeting and forecasting using computer spreadsheets. It shows what budgets and forecasts are, how they can be used and discusses their limitations.

CHAPTER 1

Understanding budgets and forecasts

This chapter is about ...

Defining budgets, budget/profit and loss forecasts and cash flow fore-casts. We'll examine the use of spreadsheet-based budgets and forecasts for day-to-day management and discuss why they are not the sole province of accountants. We'll look at planning cycles, and whether to use fixed, rolling or perpetual forecasts. Will a forecast ever be exactly right, and indeed does it need to be?

Definitions of budgets and budget forecasts

Although the terms *budget* and *budget forecast* are sometimes interpreted in different ways, the definitions we will use are probably the most widely accepted versions.

If you already have very clear definitions in your mind that don't accord with these in this book, it won't matter at all. You will recognise the detailed circumstances described later on, and the methods of handling them will be just as valid. They may just be called by another name.

brilliant definition

Budget: A budget is a statement of allocated expenditure and/or revenue, under specific headings, for a chosen period. Generally the expenditure allocation must not be exceeded, and the revenue must be achieved.
Budget forecast: A budget forecast is a statement of expected expenditure and/or revenue, based on the best information to hand, under specific headings, for a chosen period.

Let's look at a couple of examples – the first in a company department with a central supporting role, the second in a department close to the sharp end of the business, an operational role. In both cases the 'department' may consist of any number of staff and managers, or just one person.

Example 1 – Central supporting roles

The departments for wages, accounts, general administration, and purchasing might all be considered examples of central support if their function embraces most other functions and departments in the company. As part of the company's annual budgeting process, these central role departments are asked to prepare an estimate of expenditure over the coming year. They will probably need to think about such things as staff costs, stationery and computer maintenance.

To do this they'll prepare a forecast or expectation of expenditure against various headings for a given period – usually 12 months. This is a *budget forecast*, which is then submitted as a bid for an allocation of money to cover the expenditure. When an allocation of money is made – this is now the *budget*. Departments are then expected to operate throughout the year within the constraints of the budget – see Figure 1.1.

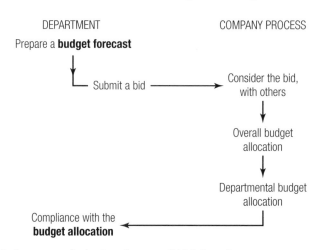

Figure 1.1 Summary of a budget forecast/bid/allocation process

It is perhaps less likely in a support department, than in one directly involved with the sharp end of the business, that there will be any need to alter the budget allocation through the year.

Example 2 – An operational role

The factory, sales team, service and distribution might all be considered examples of operational departments, for our purposes, if their work load is directly or closely related to the volume of business. We'll look at the sales team.

Sales are asked to prepare an estimate of expenditure and sales revenue, over the coming year for their department. To do this they have to prepare a forecast of expenditure and revenue against various headings. Now, while it *may* be possible in some circumstances to prepare both expenditure and sales revenue forecasts independently, it is more likely that each will be dependent upon the other in some way. For example, if sales performance is partly determined by the number of visits made by travelling salespeople, then the greater the selling effort made, the greater the cost of cars, petrol and overnight accommodation.

So we have to prepare expenditure and revenue forecasts in concert, and they must be linked by any factors that affect both, such as the costs of travelling salespeople, advertising expenditure and so on. This combined revenue and expenditure *budget forecast* is submitted to the company's budgeting process as a bid for the coming year.

In the same way as for the support role departments, a *budget allocation* is made, but in this case there will be a relationship between revenue and expenditure. Taking our simple example again, the expenditure allocation for travel expenses will be expressed as a proportion of sales revenue, and the sales team will be expected to operate throughout the year so that travel expenditure doesn't exceed the proportion of sales revenue allocated.

Because of the changeable nature of business, there is a very high probability that the budget forecasts of operational departments would benefit from review, and amendment if necessary, throughout the year. But so long as the relationships between revenue and any variable costs, such as travelling expenses, have been explicitly stated in the budget allocation, then it's not necessary to alter the allocation in the light of a new forecast.

If no such relationship has been included, then whenever sales expectations change throughout the year we must also review, and probably amend, the budget allocation.

There are of course other factors to consider, and we'll be looking at these in the next chapter.

Profit and loss forecasts

In accountancy there is a very precise definition of the word *profit*, but a general definition is all that's needed for our purpose.

brilliant definition

Profit: the difference between trading revenues and costs; that is, what is left from the sales revenue after subtracting all expenses. Money spent on capital items – things owned by the company that have a value which could be realised by selling them – are usually excluded from the calculation of profit. However, any reduction in the value of capital items during the year, which is known as *depreciation*, will normally be considered a trading expense, and so will figure in the calculation of profit.

Profit can be described as 'gross' or 'net':

Gross profit = revenue – Direct costs
Net profit = Revenue – (Direct costs + Overhead costs)

Direct costs are those incurred expressly on the product or service – for example raw materials for manufacturing and spare parts for a maintenance service.

Overhead costs are those that are incurred independently of the product, such as rent, rates, general administration, and so on.

Although we will occasionally be referring to gross profit, we will be mainly interested in net profit. In this book, and elsewhere, if the word *profit* is used by itself, it means *net profit*.

Loss is simply a negative value of profit.

A *profit and loss (P&L) forecast* shows the combined effect on profit or loss of all revenues and costs over a period of time.

Cash flow forecasts

Whereas P&L forecasts are concerned with expense incurred and revenue earned, *cash flow* refers to the movement of cash in and out of the company or department. And they are by no means the same thing. In our everyday lives we frequently encounter the difference: for instance, a salaried person earns their income throughout a month, but only receives the cash for it once a month. Whenever a credit card is used to buy something, its value is acquired immediately, but the cash to pay for it is only spent when the credit card account is paid.

Business is no different; indeed it has a credit culture of very long standing. It is fairly common for us to expect at least 30 days' credit from suppliers when buying, and to provide a similar period of credit to business customers on our sales. So the cash in and out of the business will be offset from the time that expenses are incurred – buying stationery for instance – and from the time that sales revenues are earned or supplying your product or service for instance, by the period of credit allowed (or taken!) for each.

brilliant definition

Cash flow: A cash flow forecast shows the combined effect on cash reserves of all cash receipts and payments over a period of time.

Thirty days' credit from a supplier can be illustrated like this:

	Jan	Feb	Mar	Apr	May	Jun	Jul	Aug	Sep	Oct	Nov	Dec
EXPENSE												
Stationery (£)		350	100		450							
CASH OUT												
Stationery (£)			350	100		450						

And credit of 30 days given to customers like this:

	Jan	Feb	Mar	Apr	May	Jun	Jul	Aug	Sep	Oct	Nov	Dec
REVENUE												
Product 'A' (£)			4000		6500		3750					
CASH IN												
Product 'A' (£)				4000		6500		3750				

Clearly, when we have many items of expense, each with its own period of credit allowed, and perhaps several sales items, again each with its own period of credit given, then the calculation of the net effect on cash flow each month can get quite complicated. Fortunately, it's no problem at all when using a spreadsheet.

The importance of understanding cash flow

Cash, in the end, is the life blood of any business, and there are many, many things that can affect how much of it there is in the bank at any one time. In any company there will be few, if any, managers who will not be responsible for something that impacts on cash flow.

Figure 1.2 shows some things that impact *positively* on cash flow. Positive means that cash arrives in the bank earlier, or leaves it later, or isn't spent in the first place.

Taking full advantage of supplier's credit

Minimising credit offered to customers

Minimising credit taken by customers

Minimising sales invoice preparation delays

Minimising sales invoice dispatch delays

Making the best choice between buying/leasing options

Minimising levels of sales stock

Minimising levels of raw and manufacturing materials stock

Minimising material processing times

Best possible match of production levels to sales

Minimising the period between manufacture and sale

Figure 1.2 Positive impacts on cash flow

In all cases listed, the converse of the statement listed in Figure 1.2 will have a *negative* impact on cash flow. Negative means that cash arrives in the bank later, or leaves it earlier, or is spent unnecessarily.

All this must be considered in the context of good and ethical business practice, while maintaining an appropriate quality level for our goods or services.

You'll notice that all of the items listed in Figure 1.2 are processes, disciplines or policies that will impact positively and directly on cash flow. But the obvious must not be forgotten: every good business decision will also immediately, or ultimately, impact positively on cash flow. And conversely, a bad decision will have a negative impact.

brilliant tip

An understanding of cash flow is important for managers in many different roles, for even where their responsibilities do not include direct control of cash, it is very probable that the consequences of their decisions and actions will have an impact on it.

Before leaving cash flow, we'll just consider how the *type* of business can also influence cash flow by looking at two illustrations: one that is inherently a good business for cash flow, and another that is not.

Motor vehicle windscreen de-icing products in the UK

The number of vehicle windscreen de-icing products bought during the winter months in the UK is much higher than at any other time of the year. But the manufacturer will have been making them for some months previously. In those preceding months the manufacturer has to buy materials, manufacture the products, pack and market them – and all this with its attendant expenditure and cash drain with very little being earned until the season starts.

In this example, the most significant factor affecting cash flow is a sales demand level and duration that is grossly out of proportion to the relatively long and cash demanding manufacturing cycle. The example is of course rather contrived; in reality companies in this kind of seasonal business will take measures to reduce the impact, such as having other non-seasonal product lines.

In contrast, here is an example of a good cash business.

---

brilliant example

The supermarket

Supermarkets buy their stock in very large quantities and obtain volume discounts. They receive at least 30 days' credit before they pay for the stock. The stock is immediately put out on the shelves, to be bought by customers who straight away pay cash for their purchases.

In this example, the most significant factor affecting cash flow is the combination of credit on purchases and immediate cash payment for sales.

Spreadsheet-based budgets and forecasts for day-to-day management

The data contained in budgets, forecasts, and the 'actual' figures collected for comparison, are a potential source of strikingly informative and useful information about the company's performance. I mean performance in the broadest sense of the word, which certainly includes direct financial management and control, but also such things as staff efficiency, stock control, departmental or product line profitability comparisons, and many more.

Before the introduction of IT systems and spreadsheets it was exceedingly difficult and time consuming to extract valuable data. Managers were frustrated that so much useful information, which would be so helpful both strategically and in their day-to-day decision making, could only be extracted by lengthy and painstaking work with pen, paper and calculator. A P&L or cash flow forecast rework to reflect changing circumstances, or to examine a proposed new strategy, could take literally days and produce only very basic information for decision making.

For instance, try to imagine the combination of calculations that would be necessary if, in the coming year, all of the following were taken into account in the forecast of a company manufacturing 20 product lines:

- overall sales growth for the year of 12 per cent;
- overlaid seasonal sales fluctuations of 15 per cent during the second quarter, and 25 per cent during the fourth quarter;
- price increases of 7 per cent for 63 per cent of the raw materials used for 13 of the product lines;
- production line efficiency improvement of 3 per cent;
- wages and salary increases of 5 per cent from the eighth month onwards.

Enough said! You can imagine the rest.

The use of spreadsheets has revolutionised budgeting and forecasting, relegating to the past the frustration of inaccessible information. All of the things that were difficult or just totally impracticable with pen and paper are now taken for granted, and carried out in hours or minutes. Forecasts, which were once a tedious annual chore, to be quickly consigned to a filing cabinet, never to see the light of day again, are now a dynamic and day-to-day operational tool for all managers.

brilliant tip

In order to stay in full control of our business we must forecast, test strategic alternatives and monitor achievements.

The competitive world we are in allows very little leeway for anything less than full control or anything less than maximum efficiency from the personnel and material resources at our disposal.

Forecasts – not the sole province of accountants

Some people assume that certain aspects of budgeting and forecasting can only be created, understood and used by accountants. This assumption is unquestionably wrong.

All you need is an understanding of simple arithmetic and an appreciation of how essential to our own management control budgets and forecasts are. The first of these I will take for granted, the second you will either already have, or will do so, I'm sure, by the time we have finished.

tip

Whilst accountancy skills are of course a valuable asset for any company in many ways, they are not required for budgeting and forecasting. Any manager with a clear understanding of the day-to-day operation of their element of the business can budget and forecast.

Businesses today, more than ever before, need fast, relevant and concise information to assist in strategic and tactical decision making. Producing this information requires a combination of financial and operational management expertise. It's not just a matter of 'involving financial managers in operations', or 'involving non-financial managers' in management accounting – the kernel of the issue is that all disciplines in an organisation must work together, pooling their experience and expertise, to create a common understanding of the detailed cost structure and dynamics of the business from which strategic and tactical decisions can be made.

Unfortunately, some managers resist the idea and you may hear some of the following comments:

- Knowledge and information give me a personal advantage – I'm not going to share it with them.
- They just don't understand my work.
- I have nothing in common with them.
- They can't understand my work, they haven't been trained.
- It isn't my job to get involved in that sort of thing.
- Why should I help them, they just make my job more difficult.
- What can a customer service manager know about management accounting?
- What can a management accountant know about customer service management?
- I've no problem with the idea in principle, but it simply isn't necessary.

There are operational managers for whom the regular annual round of forecasting and planning is seen as nothing but a tiresome chore which, although presumably necessary for the accountants, produces no obvious benefit for themselves in their day-to-day work. This is an unfortunate perception, but most unfortunate is the fact that for too many operational managers it's probably true – and of course it shouldn't be.

If operational managers are appropriately involved in planning, reviewing and monitoring, this will:

- create more informed plans from in house 'experts';
- broaden their understanding of the company as a whole;
- heighten and improve their awareness and control of costs;
- provide a clearer insight to corporate goals and objectives;
- produce more effective and efficient day-to-day management;
- generate a greater feeling of involvement and worth;
- create closer ties with other departments.

If your company's policy is that only the accountant's department will prepare budget forecasts and allocations, they will undoubtedly appreciate your understanding of what they are trying to achieve, and you will more readily understand the process by which they have arrived at the outcome. You will then be able to make a more significant input to your budget, and ensure that your requirements have been properly understood and incorporated.

Planning cycles

We can describe planning cycle periods as long, medium or short term. At a corporate level the time horizons of various business types will differ; similarly *within* a company the time horizons of departments and disciplines may be different. What is considered long in one circumstance may be regarded as medium or short for another.

Figure 1.3 looks at the items that could be classified as short, medium or long term. Some straddle two classifications.

Short	Medium	Long
		Business strategy
		Broader financial planning
		Outline budget
	Funding / borrowing requirements	
		Medium-term plan driver
	Product planning	
	Assessing competitive forces	
	Considering other market forces	
	Senior level management objectives	
	Longer special projects	
	Middle and junior management objectives	
Operational budget		
Day-to-day decisions		
Operational P&L		
Operational cash flow		
Monitoring/controlling costs		
Shorter projects		
Short-term reaction		

Figure 1.3 Planning cycles and periods

The long term

Where do we want to be from next year to five years hence? Generally the determining aspect for the time represented by 'Long Term' will be the 'Strategic Cycle' – which might be based upon the minimum time from concept to availability for sale for example, or perhaps the level of market responsiveness required or possible.

The longer term will show the company's broader financial plans in the context of the strategic cycle, taking into account competitive and other market forces.

Plans made in the medium term will certainly be influenced by the longer strategic view, as will management objectives and decisions at a higher level.

Outline budgets may accompany long-term plans.

The medium term

Medium-term plans are the keystone for the day-to-day operation (management and decision making) of the business. It is within this framework that the operational details of how strategic objectives will be implemented appear, hand in hand with existing products and support functions.

Every item of revenue and expense will be in a medium-term forecast, and from it we derive the budgets for the period. The medium-term plan will be detailed enough to enable effective cost monitoring and control. It will be reviewed regularly and comparisons made between budgeted and actual figures.

It drives day-to-day management and decision making – this order must be out by Friday / next week / next month, we need additional manpower in three week's time – and so on.

Elements of the long term may well affect decisions made in the medium term: is a particular expense necessary or wise when we know that...?

Forecasting and planning provide the opportunity to anticipate. In medium-term plans there is sufficient detail to clearly see if there is trouble ahead, in plenty of time to take corrective action.

The short term

In the context of the long- and medium-term plans described above there is nothing much left for a short-term plan to address, except perhaps small special projects, etc.

Short-term plans are almost *not* plans by definition: because there is limited opportunity for anticipation, corrective action or revision. Nevertheless they have a place in short projects where, for example, additional detail not appropriate to the medium-term plan is required.

Fixed, rolling and perpetual forecasts

Fixed period forecasts

Fixed period forecasts have fixed starting and finishing dates. Most commonly these embrace 12 months and are aligned with the company's financial year start and end dates, especially for company-wide and departmental plans. Such forecasts will often be used as part of an annual budget setting process.

However, it's often useful to produce forecasts for other fixed periods. For example, a strategic forecast might look several years ahead, or the independent forecast for a particular project will embrace it's expected timescale.

brilliant tip

The key point about fixed period forecasts is that the time horizon available is continually reducing, and whilst a view of say 12 months ahead will be sufficient for most businesses, six months or less is likely to be unacceptable except in the case of short projects with clearly defined start and finish dates.

You might expect that the easiest solution is to create a fixed period forecast for several years ahead, so that it's only necessary to build a new one once an unacceptably short time horizon has been reached. Well perhaps, but there are significant dangers in this approach that relate to the fundamental truth of all forecasts: they can never be 100 per cent right, and the further ahead the time horizon the less accurate they are. So, the shorter the time horizon and the more frequent the reviews and updates the better as far as accuracy is concerned. A preferred solution is to use a rolling or perpetual forecast.

brilliant reminder

Fixed period forecasts are best used for strategic planning over a number of years when they may only need to be updated annually, for specific projects with implicitly fixed start and end dates, and perhaps for budget setting purposes.

Rolling forecasts

The principle of rolling forecasts is that a new period is added, usually quarterly or monthly, to maintain the required time horizon. So, if, for example, a four quarters time horizon is the minimum required, a forecast looking ahead five quarters is created and a new one added every three months to maintain a minimum view of four quarters on a rolling basis.

This not only means that forecasting accuracy is easier to achieve with the shorter time horizon than with a long-term fixed period forecast, but it has the additional benefit of 'forcing' a review and update of the forecast each time a new period is added. As we will see later, reviews and updates are absolutely critical in most circumstances.

Perpetual forecasts

Whilst the term *perpetual forecast* is ambiguous as the technique can be applied to long-, medium- or short-term planning, for most purposes it can be taken to mean a rolling forecast with relatively short review intervals and updates – perhaps quarterly or even monthly.

The very idea of perpetual forecasts was inconceivable before IT was used in business but now such forecasts can be a practical solution and not too demanding on resources if approached carefully.

Potential disadvantages of perpetual forecasts include:

- a disproportionate amount of effort is applied to forecasting and reporting;
- the forecasts become an end in themselves.

However, there are advantages, including:

- frequent reviews and checks that the forecast is still valid;
- the greater accuracy of the first two or three months of the forecast is permanently available;
- greater confidence in the forecast by users;
- hence greater confidence, and more extensive and appropriate use of financial management;
- improved general financial management and cost control.

On balance, and with careful management, rolling or perpetual forecasts are well worth the additional effort required.

Can a forecast ever be right? Does it need to be?

There is a fundamental truth about forecasts – the only certainty is that they are wrong – which of course is why a forecaster's job is to continually monitor and refine them to make them more accurate. So how accurate does a forecast need to be? And while we're at it – how accurate *can* a forecast be?

To *forecast* is, by definition, 'to predict; estimate or calculate beforehand'.

The only reason we need to construct a forecast is because there are uncertainties ahead. If every aspect ahead were a certainty a forecast would not be needed, just a statement of what lies ahead – in the same way that a diary or calendar shows on which day of the week a future given date will fall, or when the moon will be full.

So the very basis on which a forecast is cast will limit its accuracy. Limiting factors include:

- the number of uncertain factors;
- the proportion of the number of uncertain factors to all factors;
- the degree of uncertainty of individual factors;
- the degree of uncertainty between related aspects (e.g. cost and volume);
- external influences.

So the strict answer to the first question *Can a forecast ever be right?* is emphatically *no*. But does this mean then that there is no point in producing a forecast? Certainly not!

I have often come across managers who, when asked why they don't create a forecast, say that it simply isn't possible in their particular case, or that a forecast could not be sufficiently accurate to be of any practical use. But after discussion it *always* transpires that the real reasons can be addressed and dealt with to enable a forecast to be made.

At the root of the belief that a forecast isn't possible or practicable is often nothing more than the degree of uncertainty involved, and an unwillingness to risk personal reputation on the subjective judgements that are necessary.

These factors, combined with the legacy of management accountancy as it used to be practised, will often be why there is an inclination to focus only on historic information or make forecasts qualified with 'if that happens, then this will be the result' – thus avoiding any personal responsibility for the forecast. This avoidance of the responsibility on the part of the management accountant means that someone else is forced to make a subjective judgement so that decisions can be made, but probably without the benefit of all of the information available to the management accountant.

What is required from the management accountant or forecaster is their experienced judgement that 'that will probably happen and this is likely to be the outcome', so that decisions can be made based upon their forecast. It is only by moving *towards* financial planning which requires and depends upon a fundamental understanding of how the business operates that management accountants and forecasters will gain the experience, expertise and hence confidence to make subjective judgements about the future. And they will do this – despite the plethora of information and variables facing them. Of course, that unequivocally is their job.

Having established that a forecast *can* be made, how accurate does it need to be? Consider the objectives of the forecast: what is its purpose, what is it intended to do? It only needs to be as accurate as those objectives require, with a tolerance that's acceptable to the context. The effort put into the creation and maintenance of plans and forecasts must always remain in proportion to the value of their objectives.

And finally, don't confuse acceptable tolerances – which may be moderate – with the care and attention that should be applied to creating the forecast, which must be of the highest order.

Summary

In this chapter we have:

- outlined the basic process of budget forecasting, submission of a bid and budget allocation;
- agreed definitions for *profit and loss* and *cash flow* forecasts;
- considered the similarities and differences in the process between central supporting and operational departments;
- seen that sales revenue and related variable costs can be linked in both the forecast and the allocation;
- understood why spreadsheets have made budgets and forecasts such useful tools for management control and decision making;
- realised that the most significant input to budgets and forecasts is a clear understanding of day-to-day operations;
- understood the duration or term of forecasts for different purposes, and when to use fixed, rolling or perpetual models;
- discussed whether a forecast can ever be right – and does it need to be.

CHAPTER 2

Using budgets and forecasts

This chapter is about ...

How budgets and forecasts can be used for financial management and planning, creating 'what if' scenarios. Cost control, raising finance and cash flow control are also discussed.

Our perception of how budgets and forecasts are used will be based mainly on our own experience and knowledge of our company's policies. In practice though, budgets and forecasts are so flexible that there are as many ways they could be applied as there are individual managers. So during this chapter please bear in mind that there can be any number of variations on the basic themes.

Budget management

In Chapter 1 we looked at an outline of basic budgets and forecasts, and saw how the process of forecasting can lead to a budget allocation. The objectives of making a budget allocation will usually include:

- setting maximum limits on expenditure;
- setting minimum limits on revenue, where appropriate;
- ensuring a common awareness of the limits;
- providing a basis for performance monitoring;
- highlighting the level of costs, one with another.

Because most expenditure occurs at intervals, usually monthly or quarterly, throughout the budget period, it is better to present the allocation for each heading in calendarised form, using the shortest interval that occurs between successive payments, such as monthly or four weekly. (Budget periods and span are dealt with in more detail in Chapter 5.)

So if a one-year allocation for stationery is £24,000, and it's expected that the costs will be incurred evenly throughout the year, then it's simply shown as a monthly cost of £2,000. Heating for the office, on the other hand, might be billed quarterly, in say February, May, August and November. The annual total is £3,500, but because of seasonal fluctuations each quarter's bill will be different. (For regularly recurring items like this it is usual to average them monthly, either for each quarter or over a 12-month period. They are shown as quarterly costs below to illustrate the usefulness of a calendarised presentation.)

These two items of expenditure can therefore be presented as follows:

Item	Jan	Feb	Mar	Apr	May	Jun	Jul	Aug	Sep	Oct	Nov	Dec	Total
Stationery	2000	2000	2000	2000	2000	2000	2000	2000	2000	2000	2000	2000	24000
Heating		1250			1000			500			750		3500
Monthly totals	2000	3250	2000	2000	3000	2000	2000	2500	2000	2000	2750	2000	27500

This simple layout already provides quite a bit of information. It shows the:

● annual total for each item of expenditure;
● monthly amount for each item of expenditure;
● monthly total expenditure;
● annual total expenditure.

It also enables all of the objectives to be met. Limits by item and month are clearly shown – everyone can see them so there is a common awareness.

In Chapter 9 we'll see how to compare 'actual' figures with the forecast.

Planning and 'what if'

Whenever a forecast is created it inevitably raises many questions, such as:

● 'What if the sales of this product were increased by another 2 per cent?'
● 'I wonder if that product line is doing much for profits, what if we ceased it?'
● 'What if we could reduce distribution costs by 4 per cent?'

Clearly, if we prepared a new forecast in which any or all of the 'what if' values were substituted for the originals, then the questions could be answered. And of course this is the way in which *business planning* and *profitability assessment* are carried out. Instead of waiting until the next forecast is required for a budget allocation bid, a special forecast is prepared explicitly for the purpose of examining 'what if' scenarios.

brilliant tip

Many a business has suffered at the hands of 'gut feeling' rather than objective measurement. There is nothing whatever wrong with gut feelings: on the contrary, managers' experience and expertise in the business is the driving force behind their instincts, and it would be foolhardy indeed to ignore them. But when instinct alone is applied to complex situations that could easily be reduced to objective measurement, then the perpetrators have no one but themselves to blame for the consequences. To be sure, gut feelings will often be at the root of some particular idea which is then tested with a forecast, and sometimes instinct will turn out to be absolutely spot on, but at least if the idea is tested there is objective evidence supporting it.

So, we can use business planning supported by forecasts to address simple changes – such as increasing or decreasing sales volumes, ceasing or starting a new product line, or perhaps taking on additional members of staff. Or equally, it can be used to test strategic proposals affecting whole departments or the entire company. And of course, there is no better way of checking the financial viability of ideas for completely new business ventures.

Cost control

We can't assess the overall impact on profitability of changes to even just one variable cost until it has been tested in a forecast. Gut feelings are notoriously inaccurate in this area. Managers get hooked onto one particular cost that they 'are absolutely certain' will, if reduced by 5 per cent, make, say, 10 per cent difference to profitability – only to find that when objective calculations are carried out, the reality is perhaps only a 2 per cent increase to profits.

If you link and structure the costs in a forecast correctly, the consequences of individual and multiple changes can be easily examined to see which combination produces the most effective result, and the sensitivity of each cost can be tested to measure the effect on profitability of changes to it.

Understanding the effect on profitability of each of the costs provides a properly structured 'priority list' for controlling and, if possible, reducing them. There is an objective measurement to determine which cost will provide the best return for any time and money spent on it.

Raising finance

Banks and other sources of finance like to lend money; that's the business they are in. But their profit is partly made from the interest paid to them by the borrower, so clearly, before they agree to lend, they'll want to be as sure as they can of the borrower's ability to pay the interest, and of course repay the original loan.

If a department or subsidiary of a large organisation is proposing expansion, the role of 'lender' may be taken by the Board of Directors or the parent company. Rather than receiving interest payments on their investment they will be direct beneficiaries of a profitable outcome from the proposal.

How is a potential borrower, either looking for finance to start up a new business, or to expand an existing one, to convince a lender: (a) that they are a sound investment; and (b) that they will be able to pay the interest on the money they want to borrow, or provide an adequate profit for the company as a whole?

A potential lender will want to know the answers to the following:

● Is the product or service likely to sell?
● Are the management team competent in this area?
● What market research has been carried out?
● How profitable will the business be?

- How long will it take to achieve optimum profitability?
- Will the cash flow of the business be acceptable?
- Is the amount of borrowing sought too little, or too much?

How these, and many other relevant factors, should be presented to a potential source of finance is a major topic outside the remit of this book. Here we'll just consider how forecasts can be used to support a case for additional finance.

brilliant tip

Profitability can be shown with a profit and loss (P&L) forecast. Many new ventures or expansion schemes will not be profitable immediately; it may be several years before they are sufficiently established to become profitable and repay any initial investment. A profit and loss forecast will inherently show 'break even' – the level of sales that generates sufficient gross profit to cover overheads.

You need to prepare a profit and loss forecast that extends to the point when a net profit is achieved. When seeking financial backing you should present three versions of the forecast:

1 The maximum sales and minimum expenses that might reasonably be achieved. This can be used as an expression of full potential, perhaps as a target to strive for.

2 The minimum sales and maximum expenses expected in the worst case. This determines the maximum financial support that will be required.

3 The most realistic and likely level of sales and expenditure. This will be the enduring operational forecast, the one that will be used for budget allocations and against which performance will be monitored.

Cash flow forecasts are an absolutely essential part of the case where finance is being sought from external sources, for instance a bank. They will also be required by internal backers if the cash required is significant compared to the whole company's cash assets.

The cash flow forecast is driven by the profit and loss forecast, and will show the cash demands for each of the three versions. In particular, the second version should be used as the basis for an agreement on the maximum cash that may be required for short periods during the overall span of the forecast.

Cash flow control

We have just seen how a cash flow forecast can be used to determine cash requirements as part of the supporting information in a bid for finance. Exactly the same principle is used for monitoring and controlling cash flow in the ongoing day-to-day operation of your business or department.

A cash flow forecast shows how much cash flows in and out of the business each period, and hence the cash balance at the end of each period. Now, while some of the factors affecting the balance might be difficult to influence, others may be susceptible to a greater or lesser degree of management and control. For example:

- expenditure on building redecoration and any other non- or less-essential items can be planned for a month when there will be sufficient, or more, cash available;
- ideally no more stock than is necessary for requirements should be held (the 'just in time' principle);
- ensuring that *cash in* is maximised. Factors that affect it include delays in the generation and dispatch of sales invoices, and late payment by customers.

A cash flow forecast clearly shows the impact each factor will have. While it is easy to imagine the effect of one or two factors without a spreadsheet-based forecast, in real life there are always many factors operating in concert, and properly understanding the net effect of all of them certainly defeats my mental capacity. A spreadsheet model is ideally suited to these complexities, and easily gives us a clear view of the whole cash flow picture.

Summary

In this chapter we have seen some of the more common applications for budgets and forecasts:

- *budget allocations* provide high visibility and a sound basis for monitoring and controlling expenditure and revenue;
- *P&L forecasts* are the foundation of a budget allocation, and are invaluable for business planning, profitability assessment, and 'what if' testing: they also provide for cost control, and are an essential part of the supporting information for raising finance;
- *cash flow forecasts* are also an important element in a case for additional finance and, most importantly, enable efficient use of a company's cash resources.

PART 2

Spreadsheet essentials

If you have never used a spreadsheet before, this part will get you underway, giving you more than enough understanding to enable you to use the examples and illustrations, and build your own models.

CHAPTER 3

Understanding
computer
spreadsheets

This chapter is about ...

What spreadsheets are and what they can do. All of the principal facilities and functions needed to create and use the forecasting models in the book are explained here, with examples of their use. There is also a section of handy tips and shortcuts.

How to use the example files

This part of the book will introduce the practical use of spreadsheets. Where reference is made to one of the downloaded examples it is shown as **EXnn**, where **nn** is the example number. These relate to the numbers on the tabs at the foot of a spreadsheet.

Microsoft Excel™ is the spreadsheet we'll use throughout the book and for the downloaded examples, but other types will probably have identical or at least very similar features.

We will only need to use a very small proportion of the features available in Excel, and there are usually several different ways of doing the things described. For example there are a number of ways of copying and pasting formulae, and the ones that I use aren't better or worse than any other. If you are already familiar with Excel and are used to doing things in a different way to that described, stick with what you know.

brilliant tip

Excel has very good help features if you get stuck. If there's something that you want to do, then in all probability there is a way of doing it.

There is one piece of advice that is applicable to all computer programs: READ THE SCREEN. Yes, it is obvious, isn't it? But it's amazing how quickly we forget the obvious when presented with a new screen. We look, but don't *see and read it.* More often than not somewhere on the screen, perhaps in the mouse rollover text on toolbar icons, you are told what your options are or how to put them on the screen. So, look carefully and have a play around to see what's available.

What are spreadsheets?

Spreadsheets are closely analagous to a simple principle that can be easily explained with pencil and paper. Let's take a few columns of figures, with totals at the bottom of each one – see Figure 3.1. This shows that, for example, $293 = 16 + 4 + 273$.

	16	12	125
	4	36	3
	273	200	46
TOTALS	293	248	174

Figure 3.1

Now put some labels on each of the rows and columns, so that each intersection of a column and row can be given a unique identity – see Figure 3.2. The spaces at the points of intersection of the rows and columns are called *cells.*

	A	B	C	D
1		16	12	125
2		4	36	3
3		273	200	46
4				
5		TOTALS	293	248	174

Figure 3.2

For example, the number '4' is in cell B2. This description of a cell's position is called its *address.*

Similarly, the numbers '16' and '273' are in cells B1 and B3 respectively, and the sum of them all, '293', is in cell B5.

Now, if the figures are replaced with their cell names, the sum can be expressed as in Figure 3.3.

```
293          =          16  +   4  + 273
 ↓                       ↓      ↓     ↓
B5           =          B1  + B2  + B3
```

Figure 3.3

And this is precisely and simply how a spreadsheet works. Figures can be placed in the cells, in exactly the same way as in the paper example. The big difference is that wherever a calculation is needed, the spreadsheet will automatically carry it out when it's entered in the cell where the answer is required.

For example, in Figure 3.3, if the calculation '=B1 + B2 + B3' is entered in cell B5, the result '293' will appear in cell B5.

And what's more, if the figure in any cell referred to by cell B5 is changed, say you replace the '4' in cell B2 with '50', the new result '339' would immediately appear in cell B5.

In Example 3.1 later (see page 41) you can see the columns and row border labels, and a replica of the table. The bold rectangle on cell B5 is the 'cursor' – but more of this later. I have placed the cursor here so that you can see the contents of the cell. It appears near the top of the screen as =B1+B2+B3 and is the calculation that gives the result 293.

The position of the cursor can also be seen in another way. At the top left of the screen is B5, which is the cursor's position.

OK – so what's all the fuss about if that's all spreadsheets can do? Well of course, they will do very much more, but the principles are exactly the same: figures, or calculations (formulae) expressed in terms of cell addresses, or both, can be entered in any cell.

brilliant tip

The results of formulae will always reflect exactly any changes made in cells referred to by them.

Examples of principal facilities and functions

This section summarises the most significant functions and capabilities of spreadsheets. You'll use most of them in Chapter 4 when you work through building the example models.

The subjects covered here are:

- spreadsheet size;
- the cursor, and moving around the spreadsheet;
- entering numbers and text;
- column width;
- basic arithmetic;
- copying cell contents;
- functions;
- copying a function;
- absolute addresses;
- copying absolute addresses;
- inserting and deleting rows and columns;
- formatting the presentation;
- charts (graphs);
- ranges;
- naming ranges.

Spreadsheet size

Excel has 256 columns (A – IV) and 65,536 rows available. This is far more than you are likely to need for your budget and forecast.

The cursor, and moving around the spreadsheet

The cursor has two purposes; firstly it allows you to select a cell to make changes to it, and secondly to use it as a 'pointer' to move around the spreadsheet. Normally only about 20 to 30 rows and 8 to 12 columns can be seen on the screen at any one time, but scrolling up and down, or left and right, reveals any other part of the spreadsheet.

The cursor can be moved in a number of ways:

- using the keyboard 'arrow' keys ↑, ↓, →, ← to move one cell at a time in the direction indicated;
- using the keyboard PgUp (Page up) and PgDn (Page down) keys to move a screen height at a time, up or down;
- and of course by using a mouse.

Entering numbers and text

Numbers, calculations, cell addresses, text and special functions can be put into any cell by simply placing the cursor on the cell where they are required, typing them, and pressing the Enter key.

Putting an equals sign '=' prefix in an entry tells Excel that it is for a calculation, whereas plain text should be entered without it.

Note: In the book, characters that are to be entered are in **bold text**.

Try moving the cursor around, and changing some numbers, or entering some new ones on Example 3.1 (Ex31).

Example 3.1 (Ex31)

Column width

The width of a column is described by the number of characters or figures it can contain. Each column width can be set to accommodate as many figures or characters as necessary. If the cells to the right of a cell that contains text are empty, any characters more than the width of the cell will simply spill over.

Basic arithmetic

Calculations using addition, subtraction, multiplication and division are entered exactly as they would be written on paper, using the keyboard symbols $+ - {}^* /$ respectively.

---

brilliant example

Basic arithmetic can be entered as:

      Numbers only: =(3+10−4)/2

or

      Cell addresses only: =(B6+B7−C2)/E14

or

      Mixed: =(3+B7−4)/E14

Copying cell contents

Spreadsheets very often need calculations in several places that are identical in form, but which refer to different cells. For instance, in Example 3.1 (**Ex31**) the calculations for the totals from left to right are =B1+B2+B3, =C1+C2+C3 and =D1+D2+D3. Now, while it's easy to individually enter these three calculations, it would be very time consuming and tedious to type and enter them across a large number of columns.

Spreadsheets have a copying facility so the contents of a cell can be copied as many times as needed, and what's more, by default any cell addresses they contain are automatically adjusted during the copying process.

So if, for instance, in Example 3.1 (**Ex31**) the 'Totals' calculation was also wanted in cells E5 to H5, just instruct the spreadsheet to copy the contents of cell D5 into the range E5 to H5, and the correct changes to the formulae will be automatically made. The contents of cells E5 to H5 will then be =E1+E2+E3, =F1+F2+F3, =G1+G2+G3 and =H1+H2+H3 respectively.

There are different ways to copy the contents of cells, using the example above:

● Put the cursor on D5, click the copy icon on the tool bar, put the cursor on E5 holding the left mouse button and drag it over F5, G5 and H5, then click the paste icon on the tool bar.

● Put the cursor on D5, use Ctrl+C or Ctrl+Ins to copy, using the right arrow key move the cursor to E5, hold the shift key down and use the right arrow key to highlight F5, G5 and H5, then press Enter to paste. (This is the method I use, finding it quicker and more accurate than using the mouse.) You can also use Ctrl+V to paste.

● Put the cursor on D5 (see that the bottom right-hand corner of the bold outline has a small black square), and using the mouse, position the cursor exactly on the small black square (the cursor will change to a +); left click and drag over E5 to H5 then release the mouse button.

Ex31: Copy cells D5 to E5:H5, and try entering numbers in any or all of cells E1, E2, E3, F1, F2, F3, G1, G2, G3, H1, H2, H3 to see that they are picked up by the formulae.

Functions

Excel provides many ready-made functions, designed to simplify and minimise your work constructing commonly used calculations and those for very specific purposes (see Table 3.1).

Table 3.1 Some Excel function categories

● Financial	● Date and time
● Math and Trig	● Statistical
● Lookup and Reference	● Database
● Text	● Logical
● Information	

Most of the functions are not required for budgeting and forecasting, but it's worth mentioning examples from the main categories to give you some idea of what's available.

Financial

NPV	Net present value
SLN	Straight-line depreciation for one period

Date and time

NOW	System date and time
DATE	Date value of a specified date

Math and Trig

SUM	The arithmetic sum of a range
SQRT	Square root of a value
ROUND	Value rounded to number of decimal places
SIN	Sine of a value
PI	Gives the value of Pi (π)

Statistical

AVERAGE	The average of values in a range
COUNTBLANK	The number of blank cells in a range

Lookup and reference

CHOOSE	Choose a value or action
LOOKUP	Look up a value in a column or row

Database

DCOUNT	Number of cells containing specified numbers
DMAX	The largest number matching a specified condition

Text

RIGHT	Last n characters of text string
LEN	Length (in characters) of a text string

Logical

IF(x,y,z)	If x is true then y, otherwise z
OR(x,y)	True if either x or y is true, otherwise false
AND(x,y)	True if both x and y are true, otherwise false

Information

ISNUMBER	True if value is a number, otherwise false
ISTEXT	True if value is text, otherwise false

SUM in detail

One of the most commonly used functions is SUM, and so it's a helpful one to look at more closely in a practical illustration.

Consider two columns of five figures in cells B7 to B11 and E7 to E11 that require totalling in cells B13 and E13, respectively.

One way to add the figures in column B is to type the calculation into B13 like this:

=B7+B8+B9+B10+B11

That will certainly work, and it wouldn't take long to type it in as there are only five figures. But suppose you had 20 or even 100 figures – that would be an enormous amount of typing with a very high probability of error. The SUM function eliminates the need for all the typing, and has some other advantages as well which we'll look at later.

SUM totals the contents of all of the cells within the *range* in its brackets, so putting **=SUM(E7:E11)** in cell E13 will give the same result as adding each cell individually.

Cell ranges are shown as the first and last in the series, with a colon between. For example, =SUM(E7:E11) means all of the cells within the range, in this case E7, E8, E9, E10 and E11.

Example 3.2 shows the two identical columns of figures. The formulae shown in square brackets are the contents of the totals in cells B13 and E13.

> **Note**: Things in square brackets are just my explanatory notes, they are not part of the spreadsheet's calculations.

Changes to any of the numbers in column E of Example 3.2 will still be reflected by the total =SUM(E7:E11) of course, in exactly the same way as the formula =B7 + B8 + B9 + B10 + B11 for column B totals.

Example 3.2 **(Ex32)** The SUM function

Copying a function

Copying the formula =SUM(E7:E11) to other columns will, just as before, automatically adjust the cell addresses.

Copy SUM(E7:E11) from E13 to F13; it will adjust to SUM(F7:F11). Then put some numbers in F7 to F11 to see what happens.

Until now totals have been positioned at the bottom of columns of figures, but there is no reason why formulae should not be placed, or indeed repeated, anywhere. For example, suppose the totals for columns B and E in Example 3.2 were also wanted at the top right-hand of the screen, one above the other. This can be achieved by repeating the formulae for the totals, or by simply entering the cell addresses of where the totals are in the cell where they are required. The first way just repeats the calculations, the second displays whatever is in the cell referred to, and is probably the easiest and best method in most circumstances.

We'll try both methods. For the first, there are two ways of repeating a formula elsewhere: either retyping the calculation at the new location or by copying it from the original location.

Copying is the very much easier and preferred way of course, but the automatic adjustment of cell addresses, when a formula is copied, must be inhibited. Excel has a way of creating or copying what are known as *absolute addresses*, that is, addresses that will not change or adjust to a new location under any circumstances.

We'll look at absolute cell addresses in more detail before copying the totals to the top right of the screen.

Absolute addresses

The way in which an address can be made absolute looks a little complicated at first, but only because of the unfamiliar appearance of a $ symbol in a calculation. This has nothing whatever to do with currency, the $ symbol is just being used as an instruction in the addresses.

We'll just recap on what happens when an address is copied from one location to another and the address is automatically adjusted. This is known as relative addressing, because the adjustment is based on the relative position of the new location to the old. Simply put, if a cell address is copied two columns to the right, the column part of the address will increase by two columns.

Thus if cell address B2 is used in a formula somewhere, and the formula is copied two columns to the right, the address B2 in it will increase by two columns, that is from B to D, making the new address D2. Similarly, if the same formula is copied two rows down, the address B2 will increase by two rows, from 2 to 4, making the new address B4. Finally, if the formula is copied to a location two columns to the right *and* two rows down, the address B2 will adjust to D4.

So, the default behaviour of Excel when an address is copied is *relative addressing* – the address column and row are automatically adjusted for the number of columns or rows from the original address that it is copied to.

An absolute address doesn't change, wherever it is copied to. An address can be made absolute in respect of either its column, or its row, or both. Placing a '$' before either the column or row part of a cell address makes that part absolute.

For instance, $B2 makes the column absolute, B$2 makes the row absolute, and $B$2 makes both the column and the row absolute.

Copying absolute addresses

- If the original address is $B$2, wherever it is copied to, it will still be $B$2.
- Or if the original address is $B2, the column 'B' will always remain the same, but the row '2' will adjust relative to its new position.
- Or if the original address is B$2, the row '2' will always remain the same, but the column 'B' will adjust relative to its new position.

It works in exactly the same way in ranges: SUM($B$2:$B$3) will be unaltered wherever it is copied to, and SUM($B$2:B3) will adjust only its second, B3, part.

Look at Example 3.3a (**Ex33a**). In H2 repeat the formula at B13, i.e. **=B7+B8+B9+B10+B11**, and enter **=E13** at H3. Put the labels **Total column B** and **Total column E** in F2 and F3 respectively, to identify which is which.

Now whatever happens to the figures in column B and column E will be reflected by the totals at their foot, and at the top right of the screen in H2 and H3.

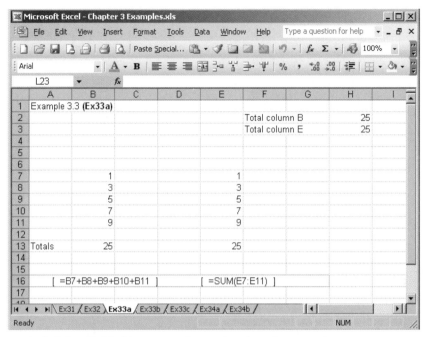

Example 3.3a (Ex33a) Two ways of repeating the column totals

Inserting and deleting rows and columns

There are all sorts of reasons for wanting to insert or delete rows and columns, not the least being errors or changes of mind, if my own experience is anything to go by! It is very easy to insert or delete rows and columns, after which the spreadsheet will automatically relabel the whole spreadsheet's rows and columns so that they still run on in an unbroken numeric or alphabetical sequence. Furthermore, all existing cell addresses will also automatically and immediately adjust to their new locations.

Let's see what happens if a new row is inserted above the existing row 9, in Example 3.3b (**Ex33b**). So far so good – there is now an extra row, the rest of the rows have been renumbered accordingly, and the totals are still correct.

Example 3.3b (Ex33b) Inserting an extra row

But what if figures are now put into the newly created cells B9 and E9? Let's put 100 into each B9 and E9 as shown in Example 3.3c (**Ex33c**). Now, what's happened? The total for column E is correct, but the column B total hasn't picked up the additional 100.

In Example 3.3c, looking at the total formula in B14 shows why this occurs. The spreadsheet has adjusted the formula to =B7+B8+B10+B11+B12, which doesn't include the new row 9, because it hasn't been told to include it.

But looking at the formula in E9, this has adjusted to =SUM(E7:E12), and this is another major advantage of using the SUM function. The last address in the range has adjusted, correctly of course, to E12. Clearly then, the new row 9 is included in the range E7:E12 and the sum is therefore still correct.

Example 3.3c (Ex33c) The effect of a new row on the different ways of adding a column of figures

So the SUM function enables additional rows and columns to be inserted whilst the integrity of their calculation is maintained. It also minimises the risk of unwittingly creating formulae that probably don't do what is actually wanted, as in B14.

If Row 9 had been deleted instead, the SUM function in E14 would still have worked properly, but the 'addition of individual cells' version in B14 wouldn't even have given an answer at all – it would have displayed an error message, such as #REF!

Looking at the formula would show that where B9 was you now have an error message, like this for instance: =B7+B8+#REF!+B10+B11.

Formatting the presentation

Formatting is concerned with the appearance of the display, both on the screen and when printed on paper. It has no effect whatever on the calculations.

There are several formatting facilities, of which one is column width, mentioned earlier. The rest are mainly concerned with the presentation of text (labels) and figures.

brilliant definition

Justification refers to the presented position of the contents of a cell within it. Text, figures and the result of any calculation can be justified to the left or to the right, or centred within the cell. By default, text is left justified and figures are right justified. Whilst it's rare that figure justification needs to be changed, it is frequently required for text. For example, if you wanted the abbreviated month labels – Jan, Feb, Mar and Apr – at the heads of their columns.

Example 3.4a (**Ex34a**) shows a sales forecast model for a number of salesmen. Note that column A has been widened to accommodate the labels.

	A	B	C	D	E
1	Example 3.4a (**Ex34a**)				
2					
3					
4		Jan	Feb	Mar	Apr
5					
6	Salesman 1	23	5	19	61
7	Salesman 2	14	67	7	2
8	Salesman 3	3	3	4	0
9	Salesman 4	7	21	38	23
10	Salesman 5	32	6	6	40
11	Salesman 6	2	1	4	6
12	Salesman 7	4	53	37	2
13	Salesman 8	76	17	15	26
14	Salesman 9	5	9	2	17
15	Salesman 10	8	20	12	6
16					
17	Total	174	202	144	183
18					
19					
20					

Example 3.4a (Ex34a) Month headings – left justified

brilliant tip

There is no need to type in each of Salesman 1 to Salesman 10. Just type
Salesman 1 where required, then use the black square at the bottom right of
the cell outline when the cursor is on it to copy downwards, and the 1 will
increment as you left click and drag it. This works for any text with a number at
the end. Similarly, for the months just enter **Jan** (or January if you wish) and
drag the black square to the required month. Excel automatically recognises
that a sequence might be required.

I have put the month labels and figures in without changing any formatting arrangements, and they have defaulted to text left and figures right.
There is so much misalignment between the month headings and the figures that it is quite difficult to see which belong to which, especially
lower down the spreadsheet. The solution is to format the text headings
to right justification. Formats can be applied to individual cells, or to an
entire row or column. In this case, because row 4 will contain only headings, I'll format the row to right justify and set as bold text.

In Example 3.4b (**Ex34b**) the headings are now properly aligned with
the figures, and consequently much easier to read.

	A	B	C	D	E	F	G	H
1	Example 3.4b (Ex34b)							
2								
3								
4		Jan	Feb	Mar	Apr			
5								
6	Salesman 1	23	5	19	61			
7	Salesman 2	14	67	7	2			
8	Salesman 3	3	3	4	0			
9	Salesman 4	7	21	38	23			
10	Salesman 5	32	6	6	40			
11	Salesman 6	2	1	4	6			
12	Salesman 7	4	53	37	2			
13	Salesman 8	76	17	15	26			
14	Salesman 9	5	9	2	17			
15	Salesman 10	8	20	12	6			
16								
17	Total	174	202	144	183			
18								
19								
20								

Example 3.4b (Ex34b) Month headings – right justified and bold

Numerical format refers to the way in which figures are displayed; remember, none of the following affects the accuracy of any calculations.

Suppose we have a calculation of 250000 divided by 52. That's 250000/52, which is 4807.69230769 to eight decimal places. But it is unlikely in budget applications that a display like this would be wanted. We are more likely to require two decimal places, which is 4807.69 rounded down.

Just about any presentation can be produced on a spreadsheet – a selection is displayed in Figure 3.4. The column used for the figures is set to a width of 15 characters, and the figures themselves are left justified for clarity.

	A	B	C	D	E	F	G	H
1	Figure 3.4							
2								
3		Examples of some of the numerical formats available						
4								
5		POSITIVE VALUES			FORMAT			
6								
7		4807.692308			General			
8		4807.69			2 decimal places			
9		4808			Integer (No decimals)			
10		4,808			Thousands separated by a comma			
11		4.80769230769E+03			Scientific (Exponoential)			
12		£4,807.69			Currency			
13		48.08%			Percentage display of 25/52			
14								
15		NEGATIVE VALUES						
16								
17		(4,807.69)			Brackets for negative numbers			
18		-4,807.69			Minus sign for negative numbers			
19								

Figure 3.4 Examples of numerical formats

Charts (graphs)

There are many instances in budgeting and forecasting when graphical representation of some of the figures can be very useful indeed. Figure 3.5 shows a screenshot of Excel's Chart Wizard.

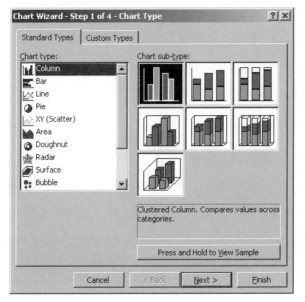

Figure 3.5 Setting up a chart in Excel

Ranges

A range, as it was used for example in the SUM function, is a block of cells that can be fully defined by its top left-hand corner and its bottom right-hand corner – see the upper example in Figure 3.6. You can also combine two ranges and treat them as one for the purpose of functions – see the lower example in Figure 3.6.

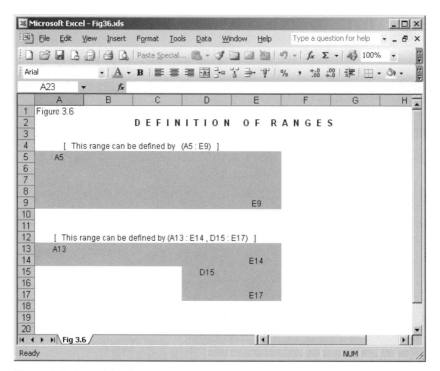

Figure 3.6 Spreadsheet ranges

Naming ranges

Ranges can be given names – literally any name you like. In Figure 3.7, the range in the upper example has been given the name SALES, and can then be referred to by name. So, instead of having to type SUM(A5:E9), SUM(SALES) can be entered. In fact, having named a range, even if you do enter it typed in full, the spreadsheet will immediately replace the range with its name.

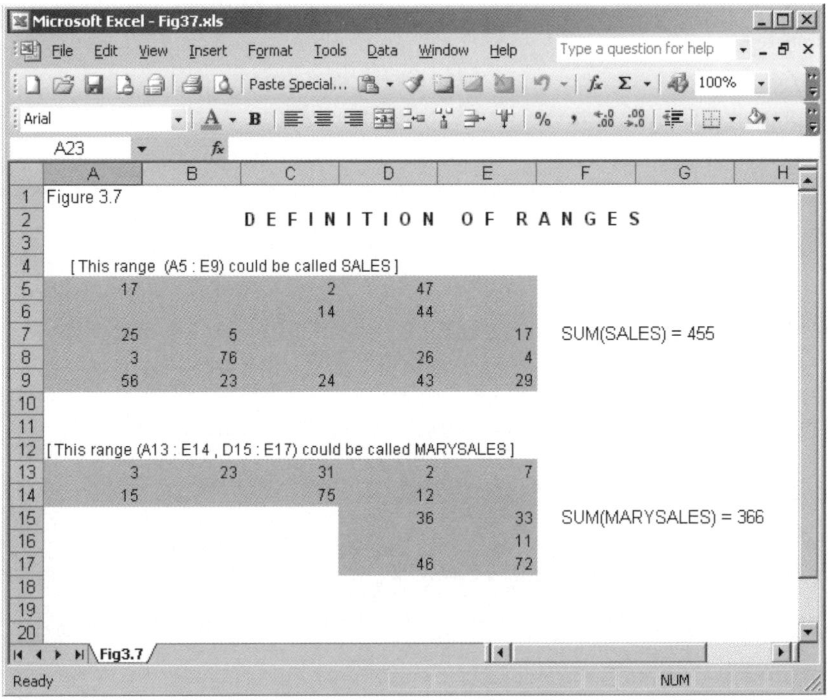

Figure 3.7 Spreadsheet named ranges

The main advantages of using named ranges are that formulae are easier to construct, and easier to understand later on. For example, if the sum totals of sales for the months of January to December are required in various calculations, each of the totals can be named JANSALES, FEBSALES, … etc. Thereafter, in any formula that requires them, instead of having to remember the addresses of the ranges, all you need to do is type the name(s). The first quarter's sales could be calculated simply by typing JANSALES + FEBSALES + MARSALES.

Obviously any calculations that look like this will be much more easily understood by anyone else, and by you as well when you look at the spreadsheet again, in detail, for the first time 12 months later! Named ranges have saved many a scratched head and premature baldness.

Handy tips and shortcuts

If you're an experienced Excel user you will have already established your own favourite shortcuts, and picked up a lot of the many handy bits that it has tucked away. If you're not an experienced user, this section on handy tips and shortcuts might be useful to you. There's nothing special about my list, it's just the way I do things, but some of them could be useful to you.

Toolbars

Toolbars on Excel are (usually) at the top of the window, and populated with a number of shortcut tool icons – see Figure 3.8. The toolbars can be customised to include and exclude any tool icons that you wish.

Obviously it's sensible to have those that you use the most.

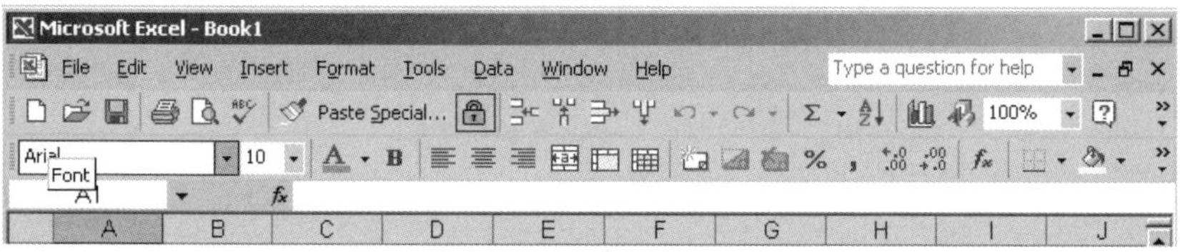

Figure 3.8 Excel toolbars

To customise the toolbars, go to View / Toolbars / Customise. The Options tab has the basic settings, and on the Commands tab you can select which commands you want on the toolbars. Whilst the toolbars Customise dialogue window is open, unwanted icons can be dragged off the toolbar: just left click and drag an icon downwards until an X appears – release the mouse button and the icon has gone.

To add an icon to the toolbar, left click and drag an icon from the Commands tab of the Customise dialogue window to the position on the toolbar where you want it, and release the mouse button.

The toolbar icons I find particularly useful include:

- Paste special
- Format painter
- Insert function
- New Comment, Show/Hide Comment, Delete Comment
- Sort A-Z, Sort Z-A
- Chart wizard
- Drawing
- Zoom
- Font style and size, Bold, Italic, Underline, Colour
- Align Left, Centre, Right,
- Merge and Centre, Merge cells, Unmerge cells
- Increase decimal, Decrease decimal
- Insert Rows, Insert Columns, Delete Rows, Delete Columns
- Borders
- Fill colour.

Totals with the cursor

Have you noticed that whenever you highlight a cell, or many cells, their arithmetic total appears on the right-hand side of the status bar at the bottom of the Excel window?

Moving around with Ctrl + another key

Note: Ctrl + <another key> means use the Ctrl key and another key at the same time.

Some of these can be very useful on large spreadsheets:

- Ctrl + End – moves to the bottom right cell of the used area.
- Ctrl + Home – moves to the top left cell of the used area (within a frozen pane if there is one).

- Ctrl + Up arrow / Down arrow / Left arrow / Right arrow – moves in the direction of the arrow to the next populated cell, or if within a block of populated cells, to the end of that block.

Arrow keys instead of Enter

When a value is entered in a cell with the Enter key, the cursor will move in the direction, if any, that's set in Tools / Options / Edit / Move selection after edit.

This will be set to your generally preferred direction, but at any time you can use one of the arrow keys, instead of the Enter key, to enter a value in a cell, and the cursor will move in the direction of the arrow.

Cell notes

Cell notes are a very handy way of making annotations and notes without any danger of affecting calculations or the normal behaviour of a cell. The size of the notes window can be adjusted as required, and it can be set to display all the time, or only when the mouse pointer is over the cell.

Paste special

The paste special options (see Figure 3.9) are available after copying something. The paste special dialogue window can be found under the Excel Edit menu, or if you have the Paste icon on your toolbar (recommended), Alt + S invokes it.

The default paste special option is 'All', which is the same as doing an ordinary paste.

Other Paste options include: pasting Formulas only (i.e. not formats or comments); values only (i.e. not formulas, formats or comments – this one I find very useful); formats only, which is the same as using the format painter; comments only; and various other characteristics that it might be useful to paste on their own.

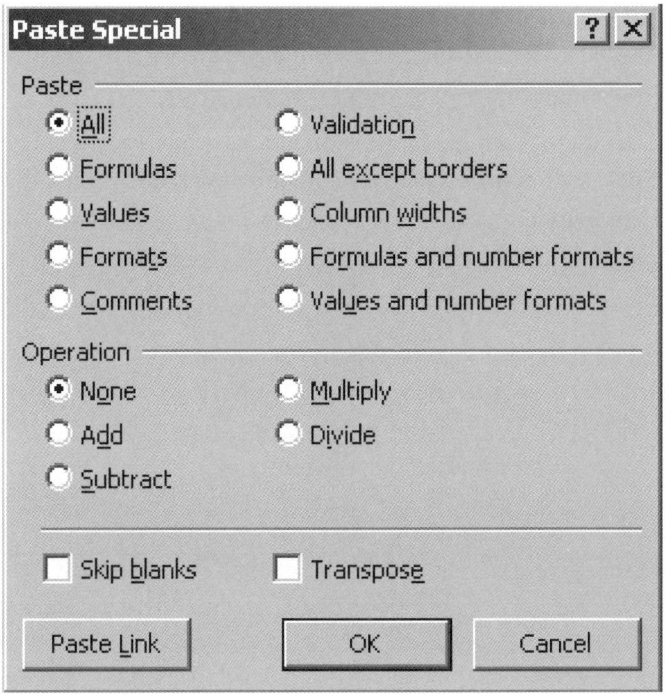

Figure 3.9 Paste special

The 'Operation' options Add or Subtract simply Adds the value you are copying to the value already in the cell you are copying to, or Subtracts the values you are copying from the value already in the cell you are copying to. Similarly for the Multiply and Divide options.

Skip blanks can be used with any paste, and avoids replacing values in the paste area when blank cells occur in the copy area.

Transpose changes rows of copied cells to columns, and vice versa.

Summary

In this chapter we have:

● realised that computer spreadsheets work in a similar way to their paper equivalent;

● learned that the intersection of columns and rows is called a cell, and is described by a letter and number known as a cell address;

- devised calculations which can be written into cells, and include figures, cell addresses and formulae;
- done the same with explanatory or labelling text;
- seen that there is a huge range of functions available in a spreadsheet, some of which make model construction easier, and others that are more specialised.

CHAPTER 4

Spreadsheet techniques for budgeting and forecasting

This chapter is about ...

The techniques used in the book for budgeting and forecasting. There are a multitude of ways and means of doing most things, and I'll describe the essential practices and conventions. We'll build the basic elements of the illustration framework, step by step, so that we can then construct the budget and cash flow forecasts that will be used in Part 3. Finally, I'll show you a number of non-essential but useful techniques.

So many ways and means

When using a spreadsheet, as with any flexible system, there are many different ways of achieving an objective. It would be wrong to imply that the conventions and practices used in this book are the best ones, or that they are infallible. They have, however, been learned and developed from practical experience, and they do work. By following them you will benefit from the many mistakes I've made over the years, so more quickly develop your own 'style' and conventions.

The section below on *Essential practices and conventions* does mean just that. Ignore them at your peril. I know, because every one of them has caught me out. Usually only once, to be sure, but that was enough!

Essential practices and conventions

These practices and conventions are to do with efficiency, the safe keeping of your work, accuracy, avoiding errors and eliminating confusion. Stick to them and you'll minimise risk to your credibility, and enhance your reputation as a forecaster. Ignoring them will almost certainly result in your credibility taking a severe knock and, quite possibly, the complete loss of many hours of your work.

Regularly save your work

This is so important that a brief technical explanation of how information is stored and used by a computer is necessary. None of this detail is essential to being able to use a spreadsheet, but it will explain why regular saving is crucial.

There are two main ways a computer has for storing information, either on a *drive*, or *in random access memory*.

The essential feature of a drive is that it is a permanent means of storage. Once information has been stored on a drive, with normal care, it is there for good. However, for many computer programs, including spreadsheets, complete drive storage is not suitable whilst they are being used. A faster and more accessible method is needed – *memory*. However, information is only stored in memory temporarily.

When a spreadsheet is used, the computer automatically copies all of the information it needs from the drive to memory. Therefore, whilst this is an over-simplification, you should assume that any changes you make to a spreadsheet exist *only in memory* until you *save* it to the drive.

Now all of this may seem very frightening. Is it really so easy to lose a lot of work in this way? Yes, it is! However, it's also very easy to avoid loss.

The simple way to minimise the risk of losing your work is to 'save' it frequently and regularly whenever you are creating or changing anything. There is no absolute rule on frequency, but every two or three minutes will be enough in most cases. It only takes a couple of keystrokes and two or three seconds, and after a while you will find that you are doing it almost as naturally as breathing.

Is saving every two or three minutes taking safety and security too far? Just consider how long it would take to rethink and recreate what you have done since the last time your work was saved.

brilliant tip

You can 'save' by clicking the save icon on the tool bar but it's often faster to use Ctrl+S.

Back up

There is an adage in computing that 'information hasn't been entered until it has been backed up'. *Backing up* means making another copy of your work.

There are two main ways in which information stored on a computer can be lost. Firstly, technical failure – all technical systems *will* go wrong one day. This means, for instance, that the drive could fail in a way that would make it impossible to recover any of the information on it. Secondly, non-technical losses occur through theft or just leaving a laptop on a train! All of this means that *back-up copies* must be kept, preferably at another location.

There are several options for making and storing copies, including:

- memory sticks/flash drives;
- CDs/DVDs;
- a professional tape backup system;
- on another computer.

Version numbers, date and time stamps

Imagine the following scenario. You are responsible for preparing a financial plan for a new project and presenting it to the Board of Directors. Over many days you and your colleagues work late into the night producing more and more refined versions of the plan. Then, in that inevitable, and certainly unplanned last-minute rush to finalise the presentation, the wrong version is picked up by someone for binding into hard copies that will be distributed to board members.

In this case no permanent damage will have been done, except perhaps to your career. It will simply be a matter of a very red face when those sitting around the table notice that what you are presenting on the screen is different to what they have in front of them.

There are many other scenarios where such a mistake can have the most severe consequences for a company, but there are two simple ways of avoiding them – *version numbering* and *date and time stamping*.

brilliant definition

Version numbering is a term used for giving your spreadsheet a file name that can be changed in some sort of sequence whenever a significant change is made to its structure. For example, if you start with PLAN01 as a file name, this can be incremented to PLAN02, and so on.

Date and time stamping includes in your spreadsheet the functions that automatically present the current system date and time. There is no reason whatever for not including both whilst development is ongoing. It only takes seconds, just once, to put these functions into their cells; after that it is all fully automatic.

Both version numbering and date and time stamping should be used. Version numbering is useful to check that the correct computer file is being handled, during back up for instance. Date and time stamping is invaluable on paper copies during development, and for regularly repeated reports. In the second case, once development is finished, the date alone may be sufficient.

Cell protection

Cell protection is a simple means of preventing the contents of a cell being changed accidentally: you can easily remove the protection when required.

brilliant disaster

Once you become accustomed to your spreadsheet, and your fingers start to move swiftly and smoothly over the keyboard – **watch out!** Overconfidence on the keyboard, as in many other skills, can be disastrous.

On a spreadsheet, before you know it, you have merrily overwritten those elegant formulae you were so proud of, and which took half an hour to work out. OK – if you were 'saving' every two or three minutes, you can recover the work. But you will still have lost at least five minutes. Protecting those cells on which work is finished will prevent accidental overwriting.

When worksheet protection is on – use Tools / Protection – cells are locked unless previously set as unlocked. There's a Lock Cell icon that can be put on the toolbar to lock and unlock a cell or group of cells.

More critically, especially on larger spreadsheets, you will find that you have a mixture of cells, some of which contain formulae, and others that are intended to receive keyboard entered variables. Whilst there are ways of organising the spreadsheet to minimise confusion about which are which, a sure method is to protect the cells that are not to be changed either during development or in normal day-to-day operations.

Finally, more often than not, only a small part of a spreadsheet model can be seen on the screen at any one time. It is thus extremely easy to delete rows or columns that you think are unused, only to find that there were entries in cells not in the current screen view.

Protecting cells foils accidental deletion of data in this way, simply because any row or column that has protected cells in it cannot be deleted.

Check sum

Despite the ease with which formulae can be copied, or perhaps because of it (that old enemy 'overconfidence' again!), it can happen that somewhere in a series of cells there are formulae errors. I have created these sorts of errors most frequently when trying out a new sequence of calculations on just one column, then, once having got it right, intended to copy all of the amended formulae across the rest of the columns in the model, but forgot to copy one of the revised rows.

Check sums, or variations, are a useful way of showing when such an error has occurred. They are based on the notion that almost all results can be calculated in more than one way. For instance, in Example 4.1 (**Ex41**) below, the grand totals '276' have been calculated by the sum of the individual totals above them, so these are column-based sums. But they could just as easily be calculated from the individual totals to their left, which are row-based sums.

	A	B	C	D	E	F	G	H
1	Example 4.1 (**Ex41**)							
2								
3								
4		QTR 1	QTR 2	QTR 3	QTR 4	TOTAL		
5	Product 1	23	14	31	28	96		
6	Product 2	5	52	13	22	92		
7	Product 3	46	9	3	30	88		
8								
9	TOTAL	74	75	47	80	276	Check >	276
10								
11	*** CHECK SUM ERROR ***							
12								
13		QTR 1	QTR 2	QTR 3	QTR 4	TOTAL		
14	Product 1	23	14	31	28	96		
15	Product 2	5	52	13	22	92		
16	Product 3	46	9	3	30	88		
17								
18	TOTAL	74	75	46	80	276	Check >	275
19								
20								
21				Error introduced				

Example 4.1 (Ex41) Using a check sum to detect errors

So why not have both? Perhaps use the column-based sum in the 'usual' place, in this case F9 and F18, and put the row version somewhere nearby. I have used H9 and H18. If there are no errors, both row and column totals will be identical, and you don't even have to keep on comparing them manually – the spreadsheet will do it for you.

If, in the lower part of the screen in Example 4.1 (**Ex41**), I 'accidentally' overwrite the formula in D18 with a number that is one less than the calculated value, the column version of the grand total still gives the correct answer, '276', but the row-based check version just to its right produces '275' of course.

In this example, I have also provided an IF function that flags up its message only when the two versions of the calculation are not the same. The IF function in A11, for example, is:

=IF(F18<>H18",*** CHECK SUM ERROR ***","")

There is also a similar function in A3 to flag errors for the model at the top of the screen.

Try overwriting a formula in the upper model of Example 4.1 and see the check sum message appear.

A similar principle can be applied to just about any set of calculations, and the bigger or more complex the spreadsheet, the more essential a set of check sums to ensure integrity.

Automatic recalculation

Recalculating a larger spreadsheet model can take several seconds. Because of this, automatic recalculation can be switched off so that when a series of keyboard entries are being made it isn't necessary to wait for each recalculation before making the next entry.

This can be very useful – but be careful. When auto-recalculation is switched off the effect of any changes you make will not be reflected elsewhere in the spreadsheet until you activate a recalculation with key F9. If a calculation is outstanding 'Calculate' is displayed in the status bar at the bottom of the Excel window.

 **tip**

There's a 'Calculate Now' icon that can be placed on the toolbar if you wish.

Example forecasts

Every company's forecast structure will be different, and choosing the main elements and subheadings from a financial point of view will be discussed in detail in Part 3. In this chapter, simple sales, budget and cash flow forecasting models are used only for illustrating the use of spreadsheets. Therefore, the main elements and subheadings used in them, though broadly appropriate, are not intended to be pro forma. For the same reason, these are neither explained nor justified here – all will be revealed in Part 3!

 **tip**

Now, some people advocate 'getting your thoughts straight' on paper first, so that all you have to do is type in the finalised layout. Well ... yes, you can do that of course, but I've never yet seen a new layout that wasn't changed very soon after it was started. It's easier to draft a layout on the spreadsheet in the first place; things can be moved around much more easily than with pencil and paper, and better still, you will immediately see whether the layout *looks* right as well.

In the examples that follow, methods and recommended techniques are introduced as the need arises, so the most fundamental make an early appearance. Once each has been described, although probably used again in a later example, its purpose or implementation method will not be repeated. This means that if you read the examples out of order, you may need to go back for an explanation.

Sales forecast example

This example illustrates the following techniques:

- file naming;
- date and time stamping;

- hidden columns;
- justifying text left, right and centre;
- cell protection;
- expanding a column width to fit the text;
- spare rows used to allow for later expansion;
- entering and checking formulae in one column initially;
- copying a range of formulae across columns;
- year totals, using 'IF' to exclude unused rows;
- check sums and warning flags;
- building in 'month-on-month' sales growth;
- integer format and elimination of unwanted decimal places.

Examples 4.2 to 4.6 (**Ex42–Ex46**) are a progression in which all of the steps shown have been completed. Try using one to create the next in the series yourself.

Notes on the example spreadsheets

If you are using the downloaded examples, you will see that all of them for this chapter are contained in a multiple worksheet file called 'Chapter 4 Examples.xls'.

If you are going to construct the examples yourself, it's useful to create a new spreadsheet named 'Chapter 4 Examples.xls' and add a worksheet for each of the examples. To add a worksheet use Insert / Worksheet from the menu bar. By default Excel will name the new worksheet 'SheetN', where N is the next available Sheet number. Rename the worksheets to Ex41, Ex42, etc. by double-clicking on the tab where the name is and typing the new name. The order of the tabs can be changed simply by left-clicking on a name tab and dragging it to where you want it to be.

Steps for Example 4.2

1 Create a new worksheet tab and name it Ex42.

2 Put Example 4.2 (**Ex42**) as text in A1.

3 Enter **=NOW()** in A2. How it displays initially depends on what the default has been set to on your copy of Excel. To format the date as you want, either choose Format / Cells on the top menu bar, or right click on A2 and select Format Cells. You can then use one of the

preset date format options, or select Custom and where it says 'Type' enter the format you want – dd/mm/yy will display, for example, as 23/05/09, or dd-mmm-yy will display as 23-May-09.

4 Enter **=NOW()** in A3. How it displays initially depends on what the default has been set to on your copy of Excel. To format the time as you want, either choose Format / Cells on the top menu bar, or right click on A3 and select Format Cells. You can then use one of the preset time format options, or select Custom and where it says 'Type' enter the format you want – hh:mm will display, for example, as 13:47, or h:mm AM/PM will display as 1:47 PM.

5 Enter titles for the spreadsheet at its top.

6 Enter month and year total headings in columns B to N. In the example columns G to L have been hidden so that the headings for December and the Year Total can be seen. (To reveal columns G to L, select columns F and M, then from the menu bar use Format / Column / Unhide. Columns between F and M, i.e. G to L, will then be visible.)

Example 4.2 (Ex42) First steps to building a sales forecast

7 Format the headings to the right so that they will line up with the numbers to be entered later. This is most easily done if you have the

text alignment icons on your menu bar, otherwise select the cells to align, right click, then Format Cells and use the Alignment tab.

8   Save the spreadsheet.

Steps for Example 4.3

1   Create a new worksheet tab, name it **Ex43** and copy into it everything from Ex42.

2   Enter the row headings as text. Don't worry at this stage that some don't fit within the column width.

3   The *spare* rows above the totals allow insertion of additional rows below the existing titles without the need to modify sum formulae. Providing that any column sum formulae include the 'spare' row, and that new rows are inserted above it, the sum formulae will automatically adjust to accommodate them.

Example 4.3 (Ex43) Entering and justifying the row headings

4   Widen column A to fit the longest row heading. As always there are several ways to do it – position the mouse cursor over the line between columns A and B so that it changes to a cross, left-click and drag the cross to the right to widen column A. Even easier, with the cross cursor between columns A and B just left-double click, and column A will automatically widen to accommodate the longest entry in it. You can do this on multiple columns as well.

5   Centre the main headings – '*** SALES ***', 'Volume', 'Price (£)', and 'Sales Value (£)'.

6   Right justify the totals headings – 'Total Volume' and 'Total Value'.

7   The date and time will look rather odd if they are now right justified so left justify them.

8   Save again!!

Steps – for Example 4.4

1   Create a new worksheet tab, name it **Ex44** and copy into it everything from Ex43.

2   Enter formulae, in column B only, at positions « a, b, c and d as shown in Example 4.4. Note that the 'spare' rows are included in the formulae.

3   Enter some sales quantities and prices, in column B only, at the positions indicated by #. Check that the results at positions « a, b, c and d are correct. If they aren't, the formula must be wrong. Check and correct them.

4   Save!!!

	A	B	C	D	E	F	G
1	FILE : Ex44.xls		W I D G E T	M A K E R S	L T D		
2				Sales Forecast			
3							
4	*** SALES ***	Jan	Feb	Mar	Apr	May	Jun
5	Volume						
6	Product 1	100 #					
7	Product 2	50 #		STEPS			
8	(Spare)			1. << Enter formulae in column B			
9	Total Volume	150 << a		2. # Enter numbers to test formulae			
10				3. Save !!			
11	Price (£)						
12	Product 1	25 #					
13	Product 2	35 #		FORMULA			
14				Form a =	SUM(B6:B8)		
15	Sales Value (£)			Form b =	B6*B12		
16	Product 1	2500 << b		Form c =	B7*B13		
17	Product 2	1750 << c		Form d =	SUM(B16:B18)		
18	(Spare)						
19	Total Value	4250 << d					
20							

Example 4.4 (Ex44) Entering and testing the formulae

Steps for Example 4.5

1 Create a new worksheet tab, name it **Ex45** and copy into it everything from Ex44.

2 Copy the range B6:B19 to C6 through to M6.

3 Enter the year totals in column N with **=SUM(B6:M6)**, and then copy it to rows 7 through to 19.

4 A year sum of rows 12 and 13 is meaningless, as they are the price rows. Delete the entries in N12 and N13.

5 Save!!! (I won't say this any more ... although you never know!)

Ex45 Check that the model works as you would expect by changing a volume figure and a price figure.

6   Now we'll put a couple of check sums in for 'Total Volume' and 'Total Value'. Both of these are already calculated by summing the rows, so the check sum could be carried out on column N instead. In O9, enter **=SUM(N6:N8)**, and then copy it to O19 so that **=SUM(N16:N18)** appears there.

It's useful to be able to display an error warning in a more obvious position on the screen, perhaps near the top left. One way to achieve this for more than one check sum is as follows:

7   At P9 (left of 'a' on the illustration), enter **=IF(N9<>O9,1,"")**. This means – *if* the value of cell N9 does not equal the value of cell O9, *then* display '1', *else* display blank text. Now copy the formulae to P19 (left of 'b' on the illustration) so that **=IF(N19<>O19,1,"")** appears there. Now, if an error occurs whereby either of the check sums does not equal its partner, '1' will appear beside it in column P.

8   The sum of the range P6:P19 will equal '0' if there are no errors, and so we can easily check that one or more errors exist by testing the sum of that range. It may be a useful aid to understanding the formulae later if a named range is created for this test, so give the range P6:P19 a name. I have called it ERRANGE1 in this example.

9   Now all that is needed is the warning flag. I have put it in B3 as **=IF(SUM(ERRANGE1)>0,"!!! CHECK SUM ERROR !!!","")**, which means – if the sum of ERRANGE1 is greater than '0', *then* display !!! CHECK SUM ERROR !!!, *else* display blank text.

Ex45 Try over-writing one of the 'Total Volume' or 'Total Value' formulae, and see the error warning appear in B3.

Note: In the illustration for Example 4.5, months Mar – Nov have been hidden so that the right-hand end of the model can be seen.

	A	B	C	M	N	O	P	Q
1	FILE : Ex45.xls			W I D G E T M A K E R S L		Check	1 if	
2				Sales Forecast		Sums	Error	
3					Year			
4	*** SALES ***	Jan	Feb	Dec	Total			
5	Volume							
6	Product 1	100	100	100	1,200			
7	Product 2	50	50	50	600			
8	(Spare)				-			
9	Total Volume	150	150	150	1,800	1,800		< a
10								
11	Price (£)							
12	Product 1	25	25	25				
13	Product 2	35	35	35				
14								
15	Sales Value (£)							
16	Product 1	2,500	2,500	2,500	30,000			
17	Product 2	1,750	1,750	1,750	21,000			
18	(Spare)				-			
19	Total Value	4,250	4,250	4,250	51,000	51,000		< b
20								

Tabs: Ex41 / Ex42 / Ex43 / Ex44 \ Ex45 / Ex46 / Ex47 / Ex48 / Ex49

Example 4.5 (Ex45) Copying figures for the year, row year totals and check sums

We now have a spreadsheet model that can, for example:

● show the value per product or in total, for any product sales volume we care to enter, for a single month or for the whole year;

● be used to examine the sales value impact of price changes.

It's also very easy to build into the model some regular changes. For example, suppose that a sales growth of 5 per cent and 10 per cent month on month are expected for Product 1 and Product 2, respectively. Formulae can be created so that only one sales volume figure need be entered for each product.

Steps for Example 4.6

1　Create a new worksheet tab, name it **Ex46** and copy into it everything from **Ex45**.

2　Make the formulae in C6 **=INT(B6*1.05)** and in C7 **=INT(B7*1.1)**. The INTeger function rounds the result down to the nearest whole number, otherwise we'd end up with fractional product volumes.

3　Copy both formulae to column D through to column M. Remember that you can copy both in one operation.

4　Now just change the starting sales volume figure for each product in each B6 and B7. The recalculated sales volume and resulting sales values can now be seen.

	A	B	C	D	E	F	G
1	FILE : Ex46.xls		W I D G E T　M A K E R S　L T D				
2				Sales Forecast			
3							
4	*** SALES ***	Jan	Feb	Mar	Apr	May	Jun
5	Volume						
6	Product 1	100	105	110	115	120	126
7	Product 2	50	55	60	66	72	79
8	(Spare)						
9	Total Volume	150	160	170	181	192	205
10							
11	Price (£)						
12	Product 1	25	25	25	25	25	25
13	Product 2	35	35	35	35	35	35
14							
15	Sales Value (£)						
16	Product 1	2,500	2,625	2,750	2,875	3,000	3,150
17	Product 2	1,750	1,925	2,100	2,310	2,520	2,765
18	(Spare)						
19	Total Value	4,250	4,550	4,850	5,185	5,520	5,915
20							

Tabs: Ex41 / Ex42 / Ex43 / Ex44 / Ex45 \ **Ex46** / Ex47 / Ex48

Example 4.6 (Ex46) Building in 'test' sales growth

Now that we have a *sales forecast*, we'll go on to build a *budget forecast* based on the sales.

> **Note:** Where spreadsheet models are larger than can be seen on a single screen, illustrations will not be presented as screenshots.

Simple budget forecast example

This example also illustrates linking between sheets (tabs) in the same file.

Steps for Example 4.7

1 Create a new worksheet tab and name it **Ex47**.

2 Enter the titles and columns for a 12-month period, including year totals.

3 Add row headings as shown, justify and set the width of column A to fit.

4 Enter in column B only:

- Formulae as shown.
- Direct costs/item as shown. (In the example, spreadsheet entered figures are shown in bold to show that they are not formulae.)
- Overheads as shown. (In the example spreadsheet entered figures are shown in bold to show that they are not formulae.)

5 Copy all formulae and values through to column M (December).

6 Enter 'Vehicle' costs: £15,000 in March. (In the example spreadsheet entered figures are shown in bold to show that they are not formulae.)

7 Enter 'Machinery' costs: £5,000 in May, £25,000 in October. (In the example spreadsheet entered figures are shown in bold to show that they are not formulae.)

	A	B
1	FILE : Name	
2	Date Stamp	
3	Time Stamp	
4		
5		Jan
6	SALES	
7	Volume - Product 1	
8	Volume - Product 2	
9	(Spare)	
10	Total	=SUM(B7:B9)
11		
12	Value	
13		
14	CAPITAL COSTS	
15	Vehicles	
16	Machinery	
17	(Spare)	
18	Total (A)	=SUM(B15:B17)
19		
20	DIRECT COSTS / ITEM	
21	Product 1	5
22	Product 2	6
23	(Spare)	
24		
25	DIRECT COSTS	
26	(Vol x Cost / Item)	
27	Product 1	=B7*B21
28	Product 2	=B8*B22
29	(Spare)	
30	Total (B)	=SUM(B27:B29)
31		
32	OVERHEADS	
33	Accommodation	135
34	Electricity	120
35	Gas	68
36	Telephone	70
37	Salaries	3500
38	(Spare)	
39	Total (C)	=SUM(B33:B38)
40		
41	TOTAL COSTS	.
42	(A + B + C)	
43	Total (D)	=B18+B30+B39

Example 4.7 (Ex47) Budget forecast row headings and formulae

The model as it now stands will calculate the total *capital* and *overhead* costs, and their combined total. But there won't be any *direct* costs included yet, because they are derived by multiplying the *direct cost/item* by the *product volumes* – and these haven't yet been entered.

It would be fairly easy to enter the *product volume* figures from the *sales* forecast into the *budget* forecast. But that's the hard way, and of course they would then need to be re-entered every time the sales forecast changed. And sales forecasts have a habit of changing!

Clearly it would be better to link the product volume figures in the sales forecast directly to the budget forecast.

Linking

brilliant definition

Linking simply means putting in one cell the address of another so that the contents of the linked cell are displayed.

Three kinds of links can be created:

- *Same worksheet* – where one cell on a worksheet is linked to another cell on the same worksheet.
- *Multiple worksheet* – where a cell on one worksheet refers to a cell on another worksheet on the same Excel file. There can be up to 255 worksheets in a single Excel file.
- *File* – where a cell on one Excel file refers to a cell on a different Excel file.

In all cases a link can be created by entering an equals symbol, then placing the mouse cursor in the cell to which the link is wanted – whether on the same worksheet, a separate worksheet or a different file. Of course to use this method for a link to another file, the other file needs to be open.

Or, to enter a link 'manually', the syntax for linking to a cell address B45 is:

- Same worksheet: =B45
- Multiple worksheet where the linked worksheet is named SALES on its tab: ='SALES'!B45

- Another spreadsheet called Salesforecast.xls on its tab named SALES

='[Salesforecast.xls]SALES'!B45

For this illustration we'll use the multiple worksheet approach – which in any case is the way in which the example models are arranged, with a worksheet tab for each of the examples.

Steps for Example 4.8

1 You can either make these additions to your Example 4.7 spreadsheet, or create a new worksheet named **Ex48**. The downloaded examples uses a new Ex48 worksheet.

2 *Linking to Volume Product 1* – place the cursor at B7 on Ex48 and enter an equals sign, click on the worksheet tab for Ex46, then select B6 – which is the Volume Product 1 for January and hit enter. The link ='Ex46'!B6 will now be in B7 of Ex48 and it will be displaying the January Volume Product 1 figure of 100.

3 *Linking to Volume Product 2* – place the cursor at B8 on Ex48 and enter an equals sign, click on the worksheet tab for Ex46, then select B7 – which is the Volume Product 2 for January and hit enter. The link ='Ex46'!B7 will now be in B8 of Ex48 and it will be displaying the January Volume Product 2 figure of 50.

4 Copy the formulae in B7 and B8 through to December. Reminder – there are many ways to copy, you can select B7 and B8 with the mouse then drag the square at the bottom right over to column N. Alternatively, select B7, hold the shift key and use the down arrow to include B8 in the selection, use Ctrl+Insert to copy, then holding the shift key down use the right arrow to copy across to column M.

5 *Linking Value* – place the cursor at B12 on Ex48 and enter an equals sign, click on the worksheet tab for Ex46, then select B19 – which is the Total Value for January and hit enter. The link ='Ex46'!B19 will now be in B12 of Ex48 and it will be displaying the January total value figure of 4250.

The total cost (row 43) on the Ex48 budget forecast now includes the direct costs, and any changes to the product volumes on the sales forecast will be automatically picked up by the budget forecast.

Linking will be used extensively in the cash flow forecast that follows on page 86.

	A	B	C	D	E	F	G	H	I
1	FILE:Ex48.xls	WIDGET	MAKERS	LTD					
2	<DATE>	Budget Forecast							
3	<TIME>								
4									
5		Jan	Feb	Mar	Apr	May	Jun	Jul	Aug
6	SALES								
7	Volume – Product 1	100	105	110	115	120	126	132	138
8	Volume – Product 2	50	55	61	66	72	79	86	94
9	(Spare)								
10	Total	150	160	170	181	192	205	218	232
11									
12	Value	4,250	4,550	4,850	5,185	5,520	5,915	6,310	6,470
13									
14	CAPITAL COSTS								
15	Vehicles			15,000					
16	Machinery					5,000			
17	(Spare)								
18	Total (A)	0	0	15,000	0	5,000	0	0	0
19									
20	DIRECT COSTS / ITEM								
21	Product 1	5	5	5	5	5	5	5	5
22	Product 2	6	6	6	6	6	6	6	6
23	(Spare)								
24									
25	DIRECT COSTS								
26	(Vol x Cost / Item)								
27	Product 1	500	525	550	575	600	630	660	690
28	Product 2	300	330	360	396	432	474	516	554
29	(Spare)								
30	Total (B)	800	855	910	971	1032	1104	1176	1254
31									
32	OVERHEADS								
33	Accommodation	135	135	135	135	135	135	135	135
34	Electricity	120	120	120	120	120	120	120	120
35	Gas	68	68	68	68	68	68	68	68
36	Telephone	70	70	70	70	70	70	70	70
37	Salaries	3,500	3,500	3,500	3,500	3,500	3,500	3,500	3,500
38	(Spare)								
39	Total (C)	3,893	3,893	3,893	3,893	3,893	3,893	3,893	3,893
40									
41	TOTAL COSTS								
42	(A + B + C)								
43	Total (D)	4,693	4,748	19,803	4,864	9,925	4,997	5,069	5,147

Example 4.8 (Ex48) The budget linked to the sales forecast

Cash flow forecast example

This example:

- consolidates the use of linking;
- shows how cash flow can be related to the budget forecast.

Steps for Example 4.9

1 Create a new worksheet **Ex49** for a 12-month period, including year totals.

2 Add the row headings given below, justify them as shown, and set the width of column A to fit.

Now, because cash flow is wholly dependent, in this case, on the budget, the cash flow figures can be picked up directly from it using links. But there are timing differences or offsets to take account of, and which, for this example, assumptions need to be made.

Sales cash flow timing assumption

Cash from sales is received one month *after* the sale. That is, the cash from January sales in the budget will be shown as received in February on the cash flow, and so on.

3 January sales value is in B12 of the Budget (Example 4.8). To pick it up in February of the cash flow, link C8 of the cash flow (Example 4.9) to B12 of the budget (Example 4.8). The link formula will be ='Ex48'!B12.

Copy to March and on through to December.

> **Note:** There will normally be sales from December in the previous budget that would be fed through to January, unless this is a new business.

Costs cash flow timing assumption

The widget manufacturing cycle of two months means that parts must be acquired two months before sales. But the parts supplier provides one month's credit, and so the cash to pay for them goes out one month *before* the sale.

4   February Product 1 costs are in C27 of the budget (Example 4.8). To pick them up in January of the cash flow, link B24 of the cash flow (Example 4.9) to C27 of the budget (Example 4.8). The link formula will be ='Ex48'!C27.

Copy this down to row 25 of the cash flow to pick up Product 2 direct costs, and then copy both through to November. (Not December, because these are linked 1 month ahead, and there isn't a January of a following year to pick up.)

Note: There will normally be sales from January in the following year's budget that would be fed back to December.

Capital and overheads cash flow timing assumption

Capital and overhead costs are paid for in the month shown in the budget; therefore, no offset is needed for them.

5   To pick up capital costs (Vehicles) in January of the cash flow, link B16 of the cash flow (Example 4.9) to B15 of the budget (Example 4.8). The link formula will be ='Ex48'!B15.

Copy this down to row 17 of the cash flow **Ex49** and then copy both through to December.

6   To pick up overhead costs (Accommodation) in January of the cash flow, link B31 of the cash flow (Example 4.9) to B33 of the budget (Example 4.8). The link formula will be ='Ex48'!B33.

Copy this down to row 35 of the cash flow Ex49 and then copy all through to December.

7   In column B enter formulae for:

- Total Cash in **=SUM(B8:B9)** and copy through to December.
- Total Capital **=SUM(B16:B18)** and copy through to December.
- Total Direct Costs **=SUM(B24:B26)** and copy through to December.
- Total Overheads **=SUM(B31:B36)** and copy through to December.
- Total Cash **=B19+B27+B37** and copy through to December.

	A	B	C	D	E	F	G	H	I
1	FILE : Ex49.xls	W I D G E T M A K E R S L T D							
2	<DATE>	Cash Flow Forecast							
3	<TIME>								
4									
5		Jan	Feb	Mar	Apr	May	Jun	Jul	Aug
6	CASH IN								
7	(1 month after sale)								
8	Cash In from sales		4,250	4,550	4,850	5,185	5,520	5,915	6,310
9	(Spare)								
10	Total	0	4,250	4,550	4,850	5,185	5,520	5,915	6,310
11									
12	CASH OUT								
13									
14	CAPITAL COSTS								
15	(Same month as cost)								
16	Vehicles	0	0	15,000	0	0	0	0	0
17	Machinery	0	0	0	0	5,000	0	0	0
18	(Spare)								
19	Total (A)	0	0	15,000	0	5,000	0	0	0
20									
21									
22	DIRECT COSTS								
23	(1 month before sale)								
24	Product 1	525	550	575	600	630	660	690	720
25	Product 2	330	360	396	432	474	516	564	618
26	(Spare)								
27	Total (B)	855	910	971	1,032	1,104	1,176	1,254	1,338
28									
29	OVERHEADS								
30	(Same month as cost)								
31	Accommodation	135	135	135	135	135	135	135	135
32	Electricity	120	120	120	120	120	120	120	120
33	Gas	68	68	68	68	68	68	68	68
34	Telephone	70	70	70	70	70	70	70	70
35	Salaries	3,500	3,500	3,500	3,500	3,500	3,500	3,500	3,500
36	(Spare)								
37	Total (C)	3,893	3,893	3,893	3,893	3,893	3,893	3,893	3,893
38									
39	TOTAL CASH OUT								
40	(A + B + C)								
41	Total (D)	4,748	4,803	19,864	4,925	9,997	5,069	5,147	5,231

Example 4.9 (Ex49) The cash flow forecast

Now, if product volumes or prices are changed in the sales forecast (Ex46), or capital costs, product costs or overheads are changed in the budget forecast, the effect of them will be picked up by the cash flow forecast.

Examples of non-essential but useful techniques

Spreadsheets have so many facilities that it can be difficult for the newcomer to identify those that will be most useful. As a general rule, applications are best kept as simple and as small as possible, whilst achieving their objectives.

This section introduces some spreadsheet facilities and modelling techniques that are likely to be useful in budgeting and forecasting:

- fixed column and row headings;
- percentages;
- averages;
- cumulative totals.

Fixed column and row headings

Most spreadsheet models are larger than can be seen on the screen at normal 100 per cent view. More rows and columns can of course be seen if the view is reduced to say 50 per cent, but then you may not be able to read the data! The Excel Window menu has two features to help – Split and Freeze Panes.

Split

Place the cursor on the cell where you want a vertical and horizontal split, perhaps immediately below the January month heading, and select Window / Split. As shown in Example 4.10 two windows appear, and you can switch between them and move around each one without affecting the column view in the other. To remove the split use Window / Remove Split.

	B	C	D	E	H	I	J	K	L	M	N
1		W I D G E T M A K E R S L									
2		Budget Forecast									
3											
4											
5	Jan	Feb	Mar	Apr	Jul	Aug	Sep	Oct	Nov	Dec	Year
1		W I D G E T M A K E R S L									
2		Budget Forecast									
3											
4											
5	Jan	Feb	Mar	Apr	Jul	Aug	Sep	Oct	Nov	Dec	Year
6											
7	100	105	110	115	132	138	144	151	158	165	1,564
8	50	55	60	66	86	94	103	113	124	136	1,038
9											-
10	150	160	170	181	218	232	247	264	282	301	2,602
11											
12	4,250	4,550	4,850	5,185	6,310	6,740	7,205	7,730	8,290	8,885	76,430
13											
14											
15			15,000								15,000
16								25,000			30,000
17											-
18	-	-	15,000	-	-	-	-	25,000	-	-	45,000

Example 4.10 (Ex410) Using 'Split'

Freeze Panes

I find Freeze Panes more useful than Split. Place the cursor in column B immediately below the January month heading and select Window, Freeze Panes. This 'freezes' the rows above and the columns to the left of the split position as shown in Example 4.11. Using this feature you can move anywhere on the spreadsheet and still be able to see your titles at the top and left.

	A	B	C	D	E	F
1	FILE : Ex411.xls		W I D G E T M A K E R S L T D			
2			Budget Forecast			
3						
4						
5		Jan	Feb	Mar	Apr	May
31						
32	OVERHEADS					
33	Accommodation	135	135	135	135	135
34	Electricity	120	120	120	120	120
35	Gas	68	68	68	68	68
36	Telephone	70	70	70	70	70
37	Salaries	3,500	3,500	3,500	3,500	3,500
38	(Spare)					
39	Total (C)	3,893	3,893	3,893	3,893	3,893
40						
41	TOTAL COSTS					
42	(A + B + C)					
43	Total (D)	4,693	4,748	19,803	4,864	9,925

Example 4.11 (Ex411) Using 'Freeze Panes'

Percentages

It's often useful to show each item of a group of figures as a percentage of the group's total, for instance, percentage of each overhead cost compared either to total overheads or to the grand total cost.

Example 4.12 shows each overhead cost as a percentage of the total overhead cost. Create these by entering **=N33/N$39** in O33 and copy down to O37, and then to O39. The $ sign fixes the divisor on the total overhead cost in N39. Format the cells as % with two decimal places.

Example 4.12 (Ex412) Using percentages on overhead costs

Averages

There are many reasons to use averages, and of course they can very easily be calculated using the SUM function; like this, for instance, on a set of six figures in C4 to C9:

$$=SUM(C4:C9)/6$$

If, however, you want to exclude blank cells from the calculation, you can use the COUNT function in place of the divisor, like this:

$$=SUM(C4:C9)/COUNTA(C4:C9)$$

The *average* function also does the job of *sum/count*, like this:

$$=AVERAGE(C4:C9)$$

Example 4.13 illustrates each of these methods, and shows the way in which each handles a blank cell (b), or a zero value (c).

	A	B	C	D	E	F	G	H
1	FILE : Ex4l3.xls							
2			(a)	(b)	(c)			
3								
4			1	1	1			
5			2	2	2			
6			3		0			
7			4	4	4			
8			5	5	5			
9			6	6	6			
10						[Formulae for column E]		
11								
12		SUM / 6	3.5	3	3	= SUM(E4:E9)/6		
13								
14		SUM / COUNT	3.5	3.6	3	= SUM(E4:E9)/COUNTA(E4:E9)		
15								
16	AVERAGE FUNCTION		3.5	3.6	3	= AVG(E4:E9)		
17								

Example 4.13 (Ex413) Averages calculated in different ways

Cumulative totals

It can be very useful to see at a glance the cumulative totals of each row to a given month, for instance when comparing actual expenditure to date with that of the original budget. One way in which this can be done using the **CHOOSE** function is shown in Example 4.14 on page 94.

To display the selected month – March in the example – the number of the month required (3 in this case) is entered in D4 and the CHOOSE function in G6 selects the third formulae, which simply repeats what is in D6 – 'Mar'.

To show cumulative totals in row 8, for example, the third function in G8 is =SUM(B8:D8), which gives the cumulative total from January to March.

> ☀ **brilliant tip**
>
> Remember to make the location of the entered month number absolute – $D$4 – so that it doesn't change when copied down to rows 9–12.

Example 4.14 (Ex414) Calculating cumulative totals

Summary

In this chapter we have:

● explored the main spreadsheet techniques used for budgeting and forecasting;

● learnt the essential practices and conventions to minimise errors and work being lost by:

 – regular saving;

 – backing up;

 – version numbers;

 – date and time stamps;

 – cell protection;

 – check sum;

 – automatic recalculation.

● created example sales, budget and cash flow forecast models;

● demonstrated many of the techniques that will be used later on, including file linking;

● seen some additional non-essential but useful techniques.

PART 3

Building the illustration framework

In this part we'll create a complete budget and cash flow illustration framework by extending the principles of budgeting in Part 1, and building on the spreadsheet essentials of Part 2.

Each stage is taken step by step, and again the downloaded examples contain each of the completed stages to help you along.

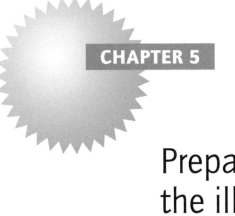

CHAPTER 5

Preparations for the illustration budget

This chapter is about ...

Whether everyone's objectives are the same when forecasting. We'll look at budgeting methods and review the budgeting process. I'll introduce you to the example business 'Widget Makers Ltd' and we'll decide on what's needed for their example budget: for example, should we have a single or departmental budget?

Finally I'll explain about cost categories, with definitions and examples, and between us we'll determine the Widget Makers Ltd forecast duration.

Are everyone's objectives the same?

The objectives of forecasting are as many and varied as those using them. Some of the typical forecasting and planning objectives listed below are regarded as general and basic – 'Inform decisions' for example – others such as 'P&L forecasting' are more specific.

- Anticipation and proactive management
- Break-even analysis
- Budget setting
- Business strategy
- Cash flow forecasting
- Comparison between options
- Control and reduction of costs
- Direct and overhead cost analysis
- Funding / borrowing requirements
- If and when an existing product should be ceased
- If things look bad
- If things looks good
- If, when and what new products should be introduced.
- Inform decisions
- Management objectives

- Manpower forecasts
- Manpower resource planning
- Materiel resource forecasts
- P&L forecasting
- Product planning
- Product sales analysis

- Project management
- Sensitivity analysis
- Understanding of cost structures
- What if analysis

brilliant tip

Unfortunately within a company the objectives of forecasting can be as many and varied as the *managers* using them.

It isn't important how objectives are categorised, what is important is that all involved have a clear and common understanding of the objectives of the forecast. In other words, before starting, the team involved in the process should discuss and agree what they are seeking to achieve. It may well be any number of the reasons listed above, or none of them. It doesn't matter so long as there is a common understanding of the objectives by all involved.

Budgeting methods

There are several standard budgeting methods, none of which could be described as an absolute best. The best solution for any particular business, department or project will be that which meets the required objectives, which may be any one of the 'standards', or a hybrid, or a system designed specifically for the purpose.

Descriptions typically associated with 'standard' budgeting methods include:

- incremental
- zero based budgeting (ZBB)
- activity based budgeting (ABB)
- fixed
- flexible.

While this list may suggest that each describes a whole methodology, in fact the differences between them are mainly about:

- how the budget figures are arrived at in the first place (incremental, zero based and activity based);
- whether the budget figures set will be altered during the budget period (fixed, flexible).

Incremental budgets

An incremental budget uses the previous year's actual figures increased or decreased by an appropriate percentage or amount based on any significant influencing factors; for example expected salary increases, staffing level changes, equipment renewals, price rises and so on.

This is the easiest approach for an established organisation or department, and is perhaps most suitable where the fundamental reasons for its existence change little over the years. Government departments and other public institutions are often in this category; likewise the support and administrative departments of commercial organisations.

Perhaps the greatest danger in the incremental approach (this is what happened last year so we'll assume it will happen again this year) is that it does not force or necessarily encourage a proper review of expenditure and revenue. Inefficiencies and ineffectiveness that are allowed to creep in over time are less likely to be discovered and corrected.

Nevertheless, given that in-depth reviews of budgetary bids are carried out, the incremental approach does provide a quick and easy starting point for established organisations and departments and can form part of any budgetary process, regardless of how it is described.

brilliant tip

A new business or project will not be able to use the incremental approach because by definition there is no previous experience upon which to build!

Zero based budgets (ZBB)

Whereas an incremental approach builds upon past experience and if slackly applied can be implemented without proper review, ZBB in effect forces review by deliberately disregarding that which has gone before and requiring managers to justify their bids in full.

In an extension of the 'justify in full' principle managers create a core budget bid which will support a minimum level of service, and must bid separately for any 'value added' component of their responsibilities, again with full justification. This approach enables senior managers to separate essentials from enhancements, and provides at least a basis for assessing and selecting enhancement and improvement packages proposed by various departments.

brilliant tip

Some form of ZBB must be used in the case of new businesses, departments and projects where there is no previous experience to draw upon.

Activity based budgets (ABB)

Activity based budgeting is an extension of ZBB. In the same way that historic costs are calculated in activity based costing by analysing the cost driving activities, in ABB the activities required to generate revenue are forecast and hence translated into resource requirements. (See also Activity based costing in Part 6.)

Fixed budgets

A fixed budget is invariable. The revenues and costs it contains are not expected to require amendment throughout its duration; the managers of the activities it embraces have no flexibility to introduce any element which will affect the budget.

brilliant questions and answers

Q What use is a fixed budget in today's environment of constant change, diversity and competition, when managers are expected to be continually vigilant of and dynamically responsive to any factors which may have a direct effect on their department or which may influence their day-to-day decisions?

A At a corporate level it is difficult to imagine a circumstance where the whole budget would be fixed, but some individual elements of it might well be. For example, elements of overhead costs could be regarded as fixed for the duration of the budget. Where a corporate budget is prepared through the consolidation of departmental budgets, there could well be a support or administrative department whose costs are for all practical purposes unaffected by changes elsewhere in the company, and for whom a fixed departmental budget would be appropriate.

Flexible budgets

A flexible budget acknowledges that circumstances which affect it are likely to change over time or, more precisely, that some elements will change over time and mechanisms must be in place to allow for change whilst maintaining proper control.

For sales volume related changes the budgetary control system will have mechanisms for modifying the budget for the purchases and costs associated with the change. For example, if sales orders for a month exceed the forecast by 1000 units then the purchases and costs in the budget related to the item by a known ratio can be automatically adjusted by the system.

On the other hand, unplanned non-volume related factors such as inflation, price fluctuations in bought-in materials and so on must be incorporated into a forecast review as they occur and decisions to modify the budget made accordingly.

Review of a budgeting process

The key processes leading to allocation of a departmental budget within a larger company might include:

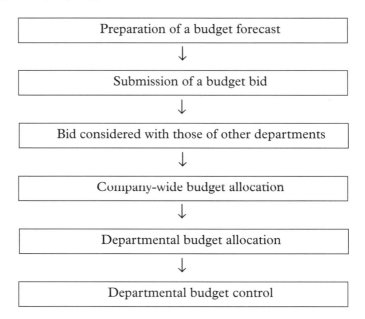

Preparation of a budget forecast

↓

Submission of a budget bid

↓

Bid considered with those of other departments

↓

Company-wide budget allocation

↓

Departmental budget allocation

↓

Departmental budget control

In a smaller company with no departmental breakdown, and where the budget is likely to be forecast, allocated and controlled by just a few managers, or perhaps only one, the process would simply be:

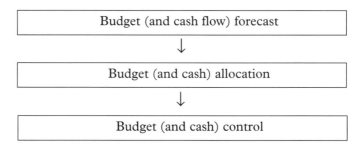

Budget (and cash flow) forecast

↓

Budget (and cash) allocation

↓

Budget (and cash) control

It is more likely in this scenario that *cash flow control*, and hence *cash flow forecasting*, would be required.

It is the *budget* and *cash flow* forecasting part of the process that we are dealing with here.

The example business 'Widget Makers Ltd'

Let's look at an example that requires a cash flow (see Figure 5.1).

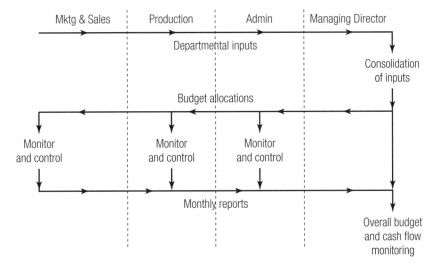

Figure 5.1 Widget Makers Ltd budgeting process

Widget Makers Ltd is owned by its managing director, who employs departmental senior managers for production, marketing and sales, and administration. There are 15 permanent non-management members of staff, and additional temporary staff are taken on for packing and distribution when sales volumes mean that full-timers can't cope.

The company's business is making and selling two kinds of widgets. Widgets are specialist components used by other manufacturers.

The managing director personally prepares the budget *forecast* in liaison with, and input from, all of her managers. She then gives each of them a budget *allocation*. Budget *control* is then maintained by the managers for their own departments, whilst the managing director retains an overview of cash flow and ultimate budget control through regular monthly figures and reports from each of her departments.

Deciding the requirements of the example budget

The first task when preparing a budget is deciding what it will be used for. Chapter 2 explored some of the more common uses:

- budget management;
- planning and 'what-if';
- cost control;
- raising finance;
- cash flow control.

Whilst it is, in theory, possible to devise one forecasting structure that will accommodate all of these requirements, in practice it's best to create discrete models for each one and link them as appropriate.

brilliant tip

It's absolutely essential that a clear picture of precisely what is required from the budget is established before modelling starts.

We'll assume that the managing director and managers of Widget Makers Ltd decide that their budget forecast and allocation will be used for:

- matching material and labour costs to sales forecasts;
- forecasting budget requirements for each department;
- forecasting cash requirements for the company overall;
- allocating budgets to each department;
- monitoring and controlling departmental budgets;
- monitoring and controlling overall cash flow.

We'll incorporate the facilities for these requirements within the illustration budget.

A single or departmental budget?

brilliant questions and answers

(Q) Should a budget be constructed as a single model for the whole company that embraces all of the departments, or should each department have its own forecast and allocation?

(A) As with most things, there is no absolute solution, but the answer usually depends upon:

- the size and number of departments;
- the degree of self-sufficiency versus interdependency of each department;
- the extent to which the principal budget authority (the managing director in the case of Widget Makers Ltd) want to delegate forecasting and control.

Let's consider each of these points for Widget Makers Ltd:

- **Size and number of departments.** There are only three departments and none of them are very large.
- **Self-sufficiency versus interdependency of each department.** There are only two products, widgets Mk1 and widgets Mk2 so each department is closely dependent on the other.
- **Delegation of forecasting and control.** We have already seen that the managing director prefers to prepare the budget forecast personally, in liaison with her managers, and to give each of them a budget allocation which they monitor and control. They provide her with a budget report each month, and she monitors the overall budget and cash flow.

The options available to Widget Makers include:

1 Prepare three separate forecasts and allocations.
2 Prepare a single consolidated forecast, and provide three separate allocations.
3 Prepare a single consolidated forecast, and provide three allocations on a single model; that is, each senior manager sees all of the departmental allocations.

Option 3 is probably best. Widget Makers Ltd is a small company with closely interrelated departments, and there is no reason why each department head should not be aware of the others' budget allocation – they have after all been involved in their preparation. And, because of the close departmental interrelation, any changes that will inevitably occur during the year – to the forecast levels of widget sales for instance – must therefore be communicated to all managers.

If all the information is contained in a single model, not only is the task easier for the managing director who only has to update one spreadsheet, but the impact of the change on each department can be seen by all the managers who receive exactly the same information.

So option 3 it is, and this is what we'll use for our example.

Cost categories

What are cost categories?

Cost (or expense) categories allow us to identify the various kinds of expenditure that are approached in different ways in a budget. Much of what follows is guidance that you'll need to adapt to your requirements, but there are two rules that you really must follow.

Rule 1: Consistency of approach within a group of budgets

If costs are not categorised consistently throughout a group of budgets, then it will be impossible to properly consolidate them for the whole company. It doesn't matter if you completely ignore the guidance here and invent your own categories – so long as they do what is required, are understood by everyone involved and are consistently applied.

Rule 2: Categorise according to use

Cost categories are about what an item of expenditure is *for*, not what the item is. So each of two identical items bought for different purposes may be in different cost categories.

Our categories

The categories that will be discussed and used in our example are:

- capital;
- start up;
- variable direct;
- constant direct;
- overhead.

We'll define each of these categories, explain what they are for and provide typical examples. Where fairly common 'special cases' exist for a category, then they'll also identified. Also, bear in mind a general reason for separately identifying categories of cost, convenience for everyone who uses the budget.

Note: Throughout the book, and especially in this section, the term 'product' means 'that which is sold to a customer'. The product may be a manufactured item, a service (office cleaning, for instance) or simply advice, such as consultancy.

Capital

Capital items are those that are not consumed by the product and which have monetary value that could be realised by selling them. They are sometimes known as *fixed assets*, the word 'fixed' here meaning that they are not consumed.

The value of most capital items will decrease with time and use, and the amount of value lost during a year is known as *depreciation*. We'll pick up how depreciation is categorised later. Of course we need to consider in our forecast the need to replace worn out or obsolete capital equipment at intervals – this is capital expenditure.

A budget forecast can also be used as a simple profit and loss forecast (P&L), and capital expenditure will not usually figure in the calculation of profit, although depreciation usually will. To be able to use the illustration model as both a budget and a simple P&L we must carry out calculations with and without capital expenditure and depreciation.

Examples

Any item that is not consumed, and which has a realisable monetary value, may be considered a capital item, for example:

- buildings;
- plant and machinery;
- vehicles;
- higher value office equipment, such as photocopiers and computers.

Special cases

In practice, most companies assign a minimum purchase price above which an item, or group of items, will be classified as capital. So, although the office kettle meets the criteria of possessing realisable value not being a consumable, it is unlikely to be classed as a capital item. (The purchase of a kettle would be categorised as an overhead.)

Start up

Start up costs are those that occur only once because of the introduction of a new product, or indeed an entirely new business. Like capital items, they are not consumables, but unlike capital items, they need not possess a realisable monetary value.

It is not important *when* the expense is incurred. Even six months after the start of the project, it will still be categorised as 'start up' if it is a 'one-off' expense and exists only because of the new project.

Start up costs, being one-off items of expenditure, will not usually be included in the calculations of ongoing profit or loss for a new product. So, in the same way as for capital items, if we are also going to use the budget as a simple P&L forecast then we can exclude start up costs from the calculation.

Examples

We can categorise any 'one-off' item of expenditure that occurs only because of a new product as start up:

- tooling;
- setting up a production line;

- manufacturing drawings and specifications;
- updating sales literature.

Special cases

A start up cost may also be a capital item, such as an item of manufacturing equipment for a new product. In this case either category can be used, but it may be clearer to treat it as capital for the purpose of depreciation, because if depreciation is included in the budget it will extend beyond the budgeting period currently being considered.

Variable direct (cost of sale)

Variable direct costs (or costs of sale) are those that arise in the course of creating or providing a product. They are characterised mainly by their rise and fall in sympathy with product volumes. If product volumes fall to zero, then so might variable direct costs.

Some businesses will have high variable direct costs; manufacturing, for example, will use raw materials or bought in parts. At the other extreme, if the product is advice or consultancy, then variable direct costs will be very low, or non-existent.

Because variable direct costs are wholly related to product volumes, it is vitally important that they are clearly identified and linked to forecast levels of business. The greater the proportion of variable direct costs to the total cost, the greater their significance and impact.

Examples

We can categorise any cost that varies according to product volumes as a variable direct cost:

- raw materials and parts for manufacturing;
- vehicle fuel for a delivery service;
- labour costs paid only for work done;
- items bought in for resale;
- depreciation – but only if the rate of depreciation varies significantly in relation to the amount of use it has due to sales volumes.
  Otherwise it will be a constant direct cost or an overhead. More on this shortly.

Special cases

Sometimes there are costs that are either only loosely related to product volumes or are so small that we should categorise them in another way. For example, the cost of sales invoicing is likely to vary with product volumes, but its total cost – in any event – is so small compared to the total costs of the company that it is best categorised as an overhead. Likewise, in the case of a self-employed consultant who is visited at his office by clients, there are no additional costs worthy of note created by more customers walking through the door. So, the consultant has no variable direct costs. On the other hand, if the consultant travels to see clients then travel costs would be a cost of sale, or variable direct cost.

Constant direct

These are also costs that exist only because the product exists, but they are not influenced by sales volumes as quickly, or to the same extent, as the direct variables. Whereas direct variable costs can become zero immediately product volumes cease, constant directs are more likely to continue for days, weeks or even months after production ceases.

Constant direct costs generally represent the ongoing investment in plant and manpower necessary for a given product.

It is important, especially in a business with more than one product, for us to be able to measure the profitability of each product or range of products. Identifying the direct constant costs, together with the direct variables, allows us to calculate the total direct costs associated with the product.

Gross profit is calculated by sales value minus total direct costs.

Examples

We should categorise costs that exist only because of the product, but which are not immediately and extensively affected by changes in product volumes, as constant directs, for example:

- routine maintenance of product-specific plant and machinery;
- full-time product-specific personnel;

- heating and lighting of product-specific areas;
- after-sales customer service;
- depreciation if the capital item it refers to is used for one of several product lines.

Special cases

Sometimes the difference between constant direct costs and overheads may not be readily apparent, and in the case of a small, single-product company they are probably one and the same. In either case, categorising the cost as an overhead will usually be your best solution.

Overhead

Overheads are costs not related to any particular product, and which are not expended on capital or start up items – in other words, everything not included in one of the other categories. This does *not* mean that the overhead category is a general dustbin, just somewhere to dump items rather than properly considering how they should be categorised. The point about the term 'overhead' is that it means 'over and above' the direct costs of a product. Overheads are sometimes known as *indirect costs*.

Overheads are the final figures we need to complete our calculation of the total cost of running a business.

Net profit is calculated by sales value minus direct costs plus overheads.

Examples

We can categorise any cost not related to a particular product as an overhead:

- rent;
- telephone;
- general administration;
- office heating and lighting;
- depreciation if the capital item it refers to is not specific to one of multiple product lines.

Special cases

While most companies employing more than a handful of personnel will be able to clearly identify overheads, in any business that has just one product it may be impossible to separate constant direct and overhead costs. Look at it another way – if product volumes in a single-product, one-man business fall to zero, then for all practical purposes the business no longer exists! In such cases, any distinction between constant direct and overhead costs is immaterial.

brilliant tip

Categorise costs according to what they are for, not what they are.

Cost headings

Having identified the cost categories, we now need to consider the individual headings within them. This is basically a matter of deciding how much to separate the costs, and how much to group them together, while making sure that every cost of the business is accounted for.

The extremes available are:

● group all costs as a single heading within their cost category, i.e. capital, direct, overhead;

● assign an individual heading to every conceivable item of expenditure, such as 'paper clips', 'light bulbs', 'nuts', 'bolts', and so on.

Clearly, whilst both extremes achieve the objective of accounting for every cost of the business, neither one of them is satisfactory. Grouping all costs within each category obscures most of the important detail; and separating every possible cost provides far too much detail and is impracticable.

The answer is to consider what is needed in the context of the budget objectives – match the cost headings to these, whilst providing sufficient detail for the purpose, but not so much that the wood can't be seen for the trees.

brilliant tip

There is one single factor that, when considered, will in most cases determine the cost headings for you. This most important element is an ability to compare actual figures with the forecast.

Why is this so basic? It's because there is a fundamental truth of all forecasts – they are wrong! Or, perhaps more generously, they are rarely absolutely right, and the forecaster's job is to continuously review and refine them to make them as accurate as possible. The way you can check the accuracy of a forecast is to compare actual figures with it as they become available. Taking in actual figures and reviewing forecasts is dealt with in Chapter 9.

Now, this may seem a rather obvious point to dwell on, but in fact it is a very common mistake indeed. All too often forecasts are broken down into headings that are both difficult and impractical to check against actual data. So, when you decide your cost headings, you must first consider what actual figures will be available each month, and ensure that their collection is a practicable proposition.

Obtaining actual figures for comparison

The way in which actual data can be collected depends very much upon the company's size and how its book-keeping is organised. We'll take a very quick look at one aspect of the way in which the books work.

There is a book known as the *nominal ledger* (this 'book' is now more likely to be on a computer, but its purpose and principle is identical to that of a manual system). The only things about the nominal ledger that we need to be aware of are that it contains a record of every transaction, both in and out of the business, and that each of the transactions is allocated to a nominal code. So, it's the ideal source of actual figures.

The nominal codes, or N/Cs to use the jargon, are often simply a set of numbers that are structured in a way that matches the categories we discussed earlier.

Nominal codes	Category of cost or revenue
0010 – 0059	Capital expenditure / fixed assets
4000 – 4099	Sales Widgets Mk1
4100 – 4109	Sales Widgets Mk2
5000 – 5299	Direct variable costs
6000 – 6299	Constant direct costs
7000 – 9800	Overheads
and so on . . .	

The individual numbers within the ranges shown are then allocated to each chosen item of cost or revenue. Taking the overheads category, for example, nominal codes 7000 through to 9800 can be allocated to whatever costs are wanted, perhaps like this:

Nominal code	Item of cost
7010	Rent
7020	Rates
7030	Electricity
7040	Gas
and so on ...	

The way in which nominal codes are grouped or structured is not random, and will probably have a significant bearing on the way in which the company's audited *profit and loss statement* and *balance sheet* are produced at the end of its financial year. Designing a nominal ledger structure is therefore best done in cooperation with the company's accountant or auditors.

So, now we can see that the cost headings needed in the budget are nothing more or less than those used for the nominal ledger. They should meet all of the required criteria – their number and structure will almost certainly be appropriate and, most importantly, because the nominal ledger contains all of the company's transactions, it is a very simple matter for us to get the actual figures that are required each month. Also, if the budget is likely to be used in conjunction with the company's year end accounts, it's worth us first looking at these and considering all of the headings in the profit and loss and balance sheet statements.

Now, whilst using the nominal ledger as the source of actual figures is easily achieved in a company that is not so large that everyone who needs them has access to the books, it won't necessarily be as straightforward for a single department of a larger company. In corporate situations there may be a devolved system of nominal codes: each department may only keep those figures it needs but forwards all actual figures to a central point each month where they are consolidated with those from other departments. This is fine – the department can also use these actual figures for reviewing its forecast.

Alternatively, there may be a policy that all financial transactions are handled by the central point; in which case the central point is responsible for passing back actual figures to each department so that they can review their own forecasts. For this system to work in a way that will be useful to departmental managers, the actual figures must be passed back to them very soon after the end of each financial period. The ability of departmental managers to take effective action based on actual financial performance is inversely proportional to the time it takes to get the figures to them!

Finally, a department may have no access whatever to the company's nominal ledger figures, or they are structured in a way that is of no practical use. In such cases, there is no reason to stop a department from inventing its own system of cost and revenue headings. It can, in effect, design a 'nominal code' structure for its own exclusive use. This will work quite satisfactorily so long as the basic rules concerning the number of headings, and especially the availability of actual data for comparison purposes, are properly observed.

Choosing cost headings for the illustration budget

In a new business of course, the needs of both the nominal ledger and the budget forecasts can be taken into account when the nominal structure is designed. For Widget Makers Ltd, we'll simply choose a representative selection of cost (and later on revenue headings) as follows:

Widget Makers Ltd cost headings in alphabetical order

- Building maintenance
- Design of Widget Mk3
- Diesel fuel (Deliveries)
- Electricity
- Gas
- Machine maintenance (Factory)
- Machine maintenance (Office)
- Machinery (Factory capital)
- Machinery (Office capital)
- Parts for Widgets Mk1
- Parts for Widgets Mk2
- Petrol (Managers' cars)
- Postage
- Rates
- Rent
- Salaries (Management)
- Salaries (Widget production)
- Stationery
- Telephone
- Vehicle maintenance (Delivery)
- Vehicle maintenance (Managers)
- Wages (Temporary staff)

This is not intended to be an exhaustive list, but shows the use of cost categories in the example budget.

Categorising cost headings

Having established which cost headings will be used, we now only have to allocate them to the appropriate categories. One way of doing this is to take each of the categories in turn, and select an appropriate heading for it.

Capital

Any item that is not consumed and which has a realisable monetary value:

- Machinery (Factory capital)
- Machinery (Office capital).

Start up

Any 'one-off' item of expenditure that occurs only because of a new product:

- Design of Widget Mk3.

Variable direct

Any costs that vary according to product volumes:

- Diesel fuel (Deliveries)
- Parts for Widgets Mk1
- Parts for Widgets Mk2
- Wages (Temporary staff).

Constant direct

Costs that exist only because of the product, but which are not immediately and extensively affected by changes in product volumes:

- Electricity
- Gas
- Machine maintenance (Factory)
- Salaries (Widget production)
- Vehicle maintenance (Delivery).

Note: Although the office space uses electricity and gas for lighting and heating, the amount is insignificant compared to that consumed by the factory. Furthermore, if production ceased altogether, the factory costs of electricity and gas would disappear. Thus, *constant direct* is more appropriate for these costs than *overheads*.

Overhead

Any cost not related to a particular product:

- Building maintenance
- Machine maintenance (Office)
- Petrol (Managers' cars)
- Postage
- Rates
- Rent

- Salaries (Management)
- Stationery
- Telephone
- Vehicle maintenance (Managers).

> **Note:** Although the factory occupies far more space than the offices, the building and its associated costs of maintenance, rates and rent are an integral part of the whole business, and they would still exist even if production stopped altogether. Thus *overheads* are more appropriate than *constant direct* for these costs.

Revenue headings

Revenue headings are selected on exactly the same principle as those for cost headings. The nominal ledger is the first place we look for guidance; the number of headings should be appropriate to the need and, of course, being able to compare actual performance with forecast is of paramount importance.

If a budget is driven by sales volumes, as the illustration budget will be, then the revenue headings should be aligned with them. So, if there are two products' sales volumes in the budget, then there must be two matching revenue headings. And exactly the same rationale applies if one of the requirements of the model is to assess the individual profitability of products – matched cost and revenue headings are needed.

In the case of Widget Makers Ltd, there will be two products' sales volumes driving the budget – Widgets Mk1 and Widgets Mk2 – and so two matching revenue headings are needed:

- Widgets Mk1
- Widgets Mk2.

The forecast's duration and periods

Duration and starting point

We can make budget forecast for any length of time, although one year is most commonly used. For long-term business planning several years may be required, and we can do this either by creating a single model of the required duration, say five years, or by building five separate, but linked, one-year models. In almost every case, the latter is best for size and manageability.

brilliant tip

The trick is to concentrate entirely on the first year until you are sure that the model meets your needs, then simply extend it, which only takes a few minutes, and there you are – a five-year business plan!

For Widget Makers Ltd we'll create a one-year forecast. Again, the forecast can start at any point in the calendar but it's best to align it with the company's financial year, whatever that may be – from 1 January to 31 December for example.

Widget Makers Ltd starts its financial year on 1 January.

The number of periods

Within the span of a forecast, we can use any number of periods. However, the number of periods, just like the cost and revenue headings, must be aligned with the way in which actual figures are obtained.

Quite simply, if, for example, the nominal ledger uses 12 calendar monthly periods in a year, then the budget's periods must be aligned with them. Some companies prefer to use 13 fixed periods of four weeks because they find this suits them better.

Summary

In this chapter all of the preparatory work for creating a budget forecast has been done. We have also:

● defined the budgeting process for Widget Makers Ltd;

● defined the objectives and requirements of the budget forecast:

  – matching material and labour costs to sales forecasts;

  – forecasting budget requirements for each department;

  – forecasting cash requirements for the company overall;

  – allocating budgets to each department;

  – monitoring and controlling departmental budgets;

  – monitoring and controlling overall cash flow.

● decided on a single budget model that everyone will use rather than an individual one for each department;

● understood the cost and revenue categories, and looked at some examples;

● realised that the nominal ledger is the first place to look for a list of cost and revenue headings, but there are also other ways of getting this information;

● assigned the cost headings chosen for Widget Makers Ltd to their categories;

● discussed forecast duration and periods; a one-year span with 12 calendar monthly periods was decided as best for Widget Makers Ltd.

Creating the illustration framework

This chapter is about ...

Creating the complete illustration framework comprising a sales, budget and cash flow forecast.

> **Important:** I recommend you use the ready made illustration framework available with the downloaded examples, rather than build one yourself. However, I'll give you enough detail in this chapter if you want to create your own examples. Also note that the downloaded examples contain some features that will be used later in the book – ignore these for now.

The sales forecast

The downloaded example is the Sales Forecast tab of Chapter 6 Illustration Framework.xls. Below row 21 it contains features used later in the book – ignore these for now.

Creating the sales forecast (build it yourself)

1 The first job is to create a new spreadsheet Chapter 6 Illustration Framework, and name the first tab 'Sales Forecast' (see Figures 6.1 and 6.2).

2 Copy Example 4.6 (**Ex46**) into the tab 'Sales Forecast'.

3 Change all of the row titles that are 'Product 1' and 'Product 2' to 'Widgets Mk1' and 'Widgets Mk2' respectively.

4 Leave the figures that already exist as they are. Although they will be changed in due course, they will do for now to test the system as it is created. (If you have already taken them out – put them back please!)

And that's it.

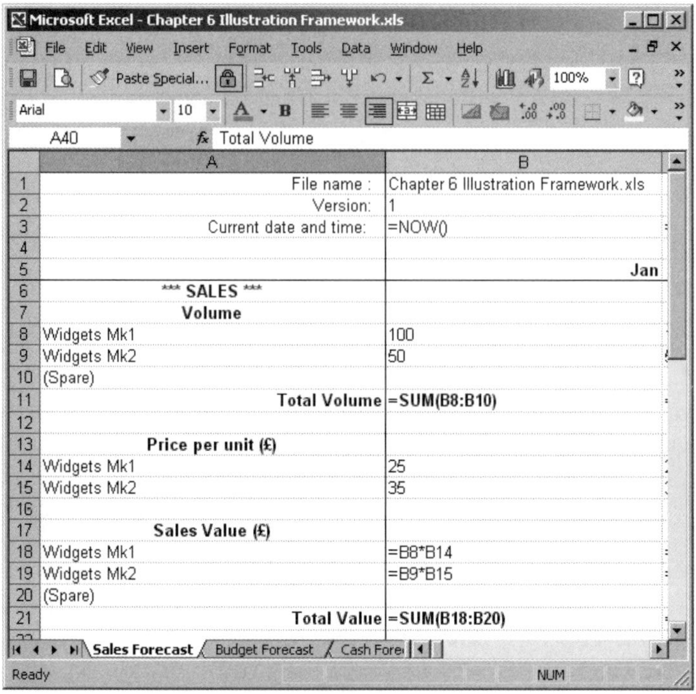

Figure 6.1 Sales forecast formula display

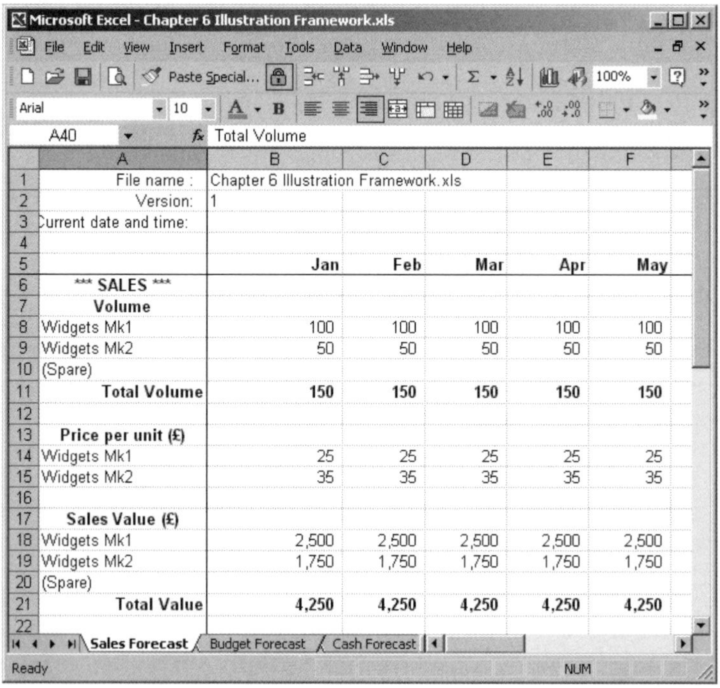

Figure 6.2 Sales forecast normal display

The budget forecast

The downloaded example is the Budget Forecast tab of Chapter 6 Illustration Framework.xls. Below row 69 it contains features used later in the book – ignore these for now.

Creating the budget forecast (build it yourself)

Figure 6.4 (later) shows how the completed budget forecast will look. The columns for February to November have been hidden so that the year total and check sums can be seen.

1 Create a tab named Budget Forecast in the Illustration Framework spreadsheet.

2 Create month headings in columns B to M, and Year in column N.

3 Enter the row headings shown in Figure 6.3.

	A	B
1	File name :	Chapter 6 Illustration Framework.xls
2	Version:	1
3	Current date and time:	=NOW()
4	=IF(INT(SUM(CHECKOUT))<>INT(N69),"!!!! CHECK SUM ERROR !!!!",""	
5	Click here to jump to the charts	
6		Jan
7	Sales	
8	Volume - Widgets Mk1	='Sales Forecast'!B8
9	Volume - Widgets Mk2	='Sales Forecast'!B9
10	(Spare)	
11	Total volume	=SUM(B8:B10)
12		
13	Value - Widgets Mk1	='Sales Forecast'!B18
14	Value - Widgets Mk2	='Sales Forecast'!B19
15	(Spare)	
16	Total £ Value	=SUM(B13:B15)
17		
18	Capital Costs	
19	Factory machinery	
20	Office machinery	
21	(Spare)	
22	Total (A)	=SUM(B19:B21)
23		
24	Start Up Costs	
25	Design of Widget Mk3	
26	(Spare)	
27	Total (B)	=SUM(B25:B26)
28		
29	Variable Direct Costs / Item	
30	Parts for Widgets Mk1	5
31	Parts for Widgets Mk2	6
32	Diesel fuel (Deliveries)	
33	Wages (Temporary staff)	
34	(Spare)	
35		

Figure 6.3 Budget forecast formula display

36	**Variable Direct Costs**	
37	(Vol x Cost / Item)	
38	Parts for Widgets Mk1	=B8*B30
39	Parts for Widgets Mk2	=B9*B31
40	Diesel fuel (Deliveries)	=B$11*B32
41	Wages (Temporary staff)	=B$11*B33
42	(Spare)	
43	Total (C)	=SUM(B38:B42)
44		
45	**Constant Direct Costs**	
46	Electricity	
47	Gas	
48	Machine maintenance (Factory)	
49	Salaries (Widget production)	
50	Vehicle maintenance (Delivery)	
51	(Spare)	
52	Total (D)	=SUM(B46:B51)
53		
54	**Overheads**	
55	Building maintenance	
56	Machine maintenance (Office)	
57	Petrol (Manager's cars)	
58	Postage	
59	Rates	
60	Salaries (Management)	
61	Stationery	
62	Telephone	
63	Vehicle maintenance (Managers)	
64	(Spare)	
65	Total (E)	=SUM(B55:B64)
66		
67	**Total Costs**	
68	(A+B+C+D+E)	
69	Total (F)	=B22+B27+B43+B52+B65

Figure 6.3 Continued

4 Enter the formula shown in Figure 6.3. (This display of the formulae in cells can be switched on with Tools / Formula Auditing / Formula Auditing Mode, or with Ctrl + `.)

5 Copy the formula across to column N (Month 12).

6 Error detecting check sums are needed. There are many ways to perform a check sum, of course. In this case I have chosen to have a separate check for each of the cost category blocks, and then add all of them together for comparison with the full year total costs. I have then put a check sum warning flag near the top left of the spreadsheet where it is most likely to be seen.

The steps for the check sum are:

- Create a named range that embraces all of the cells for each of the cost category blocks. For example, the ranges and names given to them in the downloaded illustration framework are:

Cost category block	Range	Name of created range
CAPITAL	B19:M21	CAPITAL
START UP COSTS	B25:M26	STARTUP
VARIABLE DIRECT COSTS	B38:M42	VARIABLE
CONSTANT DIRECT COSTS	B46:M51	CONSTANT
OVERHEADS	B55:M64	OVERHEADS

- Enter a SUM formulae for each of the ranges, in column P, as follows:

In cell	Enter
P22	=SUM(CAPITAL)
P27	=SUM(STARTUP)
P43	=SUM(VARIABLE)
P52	=SUM(CONSTANT)
P65	=SUM(OVERHEADS)

- We now need to add up all of these SUMs. I have done it by creating another named range 'Checkout', which is P22:P65, and putting **=SUM(CHECKOUT)** in P69. This calculation should be the same as the year total costs in N69.

- Finally, it is useful to have a warning message appear somewhere easily seen if the two totals are not the same. I have put it in A4, using the formulae:

  =IF(INT(SUM(CHECKOUT))<>INT(N69),"!!!!   CHECK SUM ERROR !!!!","")

  A4 will be blank if everything adds up properly or it will display the message "!!!! CHECK SUM ERROR !!!!" if not.

That completes work on the budget forecast framework as shown in Figure 6.3 until real values are entered later on.

	A	B	M	N	O	P
1	File name :	Chapter 6 Illustration Framework.xls				
2	Version:	1				
3	Current date and time:					
4						
5	Click here to jump to the charts			Year		Check
6		Jan	Dec	Total		Sums
7	**Sales**					
8	Volume - Widgets Mk1	100	100	1,200		
9	Volume - Widgets Mk2	50	50	600		
10	(Spare)			0		
11	Total volume	150	150	1,800		
12						
13	Value - Widgets Mk1	2,500	2,500	30,000		
14	Value - Widgets Mk2	1,750	1,750	21,000		
15	(Spare)			0		
16	Total £ Value	4,250	4,250	51,000		
17						
18	**Capital Costs**					
19	Factory machinery			15,000		
20	Office machinery			30,000		
21	(Spare)			0		
22	Total (A)	0	0	45,000		45,000
23						
24	**Start Up Costs**					
25	Design of Widget Mk3			0		
26	(Spare)			0		
27	Total (B)	0	0	0		0
28						
29	**Variable Direct Costs / Item**					
30	Parts for Widgets Mk1	5	5			
31	Parts for Widgets Mk2	6	6			
32	Diesel fuel (Deliveries)					
33	Wages (Temporary staff)					
34	(Spare)					
35						

Figure 6.4 Budget forecast normal display, columns C–L hidden

36	**Variable Direct Costs**				
37	(Vol x Cost / Item)				
38	Parts for Widgets Mk1	500	500	**6,000**	
39	Parts for Widgets Mk2	300	300	**3,600**	
40	Diesel fuel (Deliveries)	0	0	**0**	
41	Wages (Temporary staff)	0	0	**0**	
42	(Spare)			**0**	
43	Total (C)	800	800	**9,600**	9,600
44					
45	**Constant Direct Costs**				
46	Electricity			**0**	
47	Gas			**0**	
48	Machine maintenance (Factory)			**0**	
49	Salaries (Widget production)			**0**	
50	Vehicle maintenance (Delivery)			**0**	
51	(Spare)			**0**	
52	Total (D)	0	0	**0**	0
53					
54	**Overheads**				
55	Building maintenance			**0**	
56	Machine maintenance (Office)			**0**	
57	Petrol (Manager's cars)			**0**	
58	Postage			**0**	
59	Rates			**0**	
60	Salaries (Management)			**0**	
61	Stationery			**0**	
62	Telephone			**0**	
63	Vehicle maintenance (Managers)			**0**	
64	(Spare)			**0**	
65	Total (E)	0	0	**0**	0
66					
67	**Total Costs**				
68	(A+B+C+D+E)				
69	Total (F)	800	800	**54,600**	54,600

Figure 6.4 Continued

The cash flow forecast

The downloaded example is the Cash Forecast tab of Chapter 6 Illustration Framework.xls. Below row 66 it contains features used later in the book – ignore these for now.

A cash flow forecast is not always required and it's less likely to be used the further the controller of the budget is from the controller of the company's cash flow – the person who actually sends out sales invoices and makes payments. But, of course, before the advent of computers in business, it was difficult enough for even one person to fully understand the cash flow.

Nowadays, however, it really is very easy indeed for budget controllers to understand and keep track of the cash flow generated by their budget. And by doing so, they will be making their contribution to the company's overall cash resources. Consider the impact of say ten departments in a middle size company improving cash flow by just 5 per cent each.

VAT

Because some users will not be concerned with VAT, although it's a vital aspect for those who are, it will be considered only after the whole illustration system is complete.

Back to Widget Makers Ltd, who most certainly do need to monitor and control their cash. In the same way as for the budget, the cash flow forecast illustrations are presented in both 'formulae' and 'normal' display formats.

Figure 6.6 (later) shows how the finished cash forecast will look. Note that months March to December have been hidden for the sake of clarity.

brilliant tip

The fundamental difference between a budget forecast and a cash flow forecast is *timing* and, therefore, an offset between the budget and cash flow needs to be built in.

An offset is very easily provided. For instance, if we want March 'Sales' – which are in column D – to appear as 'Cash In' for April – which is column E – it's only necessary to link column E of the cash flow to column D of the budget.

Clearly the offsets used in the example are only illustrative. In this area, more than any other, they are very much dependent upon the company's policy, the nature of its business, and the policy and behaviour of it's customers and suppliers.

In our example then, offsets will be based on credible possibilities and explained as such, but we'll avoid unnecessary complexities.

Creating the cash flow forecast (build it yourself)

1 Create a tab named Cash Forecast in the Illustration Framework spreadsheet.

2 Create month headings in columns B to M, and Year in column N.

3 Enter the row headings shown in Figure 6.5. (This display of the formulae in cells can be switched on with Tools / Formula Auditing / Formula Auditing Mode, or with Ctrl`.)

4 Copy the formula across to column N (Month 12).

	A	B	C
1	File name :	Chapter 6 Illustration Frame	
2	Version:	1	
3	Current date and time:	=NOW()	=NOW()
4	=IF(TRUNC(N61)<>TRUNC(P61),"!!!! CHECK SUM ERROR !!!!",		
5	Click here to jump the charts		
6		Jan	Feb
7			
8	**Cash In**		
9	From sales - Widgets Mk1		='Budget Forecast'!B13
10	From sales - Widgets Mk2		='Budget Forecast'!B14
11	(Spare)		='Budget Forecast'!B15
12	Total Cash In	=SUM(B9:B11)	=SUM(C9:C11)
13			
14	**Cash out - Capital**		
15	Factory machinery	='Budget Forecast'!B19	='Budget Forecast'!C19
16	Office machinery	='Budget Forecast'!B20	='Budget Forecast'!C20
17	(Spare)	='Budget Forecast'!B21	='Budget Forecast'!C21
18	Total (A)	=SUM(B15:B17)	=SUM(C15:C17)
19			
20	**Cash Out - Startup**		
21	Design of Widget Mk3	='Budget Forecast'!B25	='Budget Forecast'!C25
22	(Spare)	='Budget Forecast'!B26	='Budget Forecast'!C26
23	Total (B)	=SUM(B21:B22)	=SUM(C21:C22)
24			
25	**Cash Out - Variable Direct**		
26	Parts for Widgets Mk1	='Budget Forecast'!C38	='Budget Forecast'!D38
27	Parts for Widgets Mk2	='Budget Forecast'!C39	='Budget Forecast'!D39
28	Diesel fuel (Deliveries)	=C28	='Budget Forecast'!C40
29	Wages (Temporary staff)	='Budget Forecast'!B41	='Budget Forecast'!C41
30	(Spare)		
31	Total (C)	=SUM(B26:B30)	=SUM(C26:C30)
32			
33	**Cash Out - Constant Direct**		
34	Electricity	='Budget Forecast'!B46	='Budget Forecast'!C46
35	Gas	='Budget Forecast'!B47	='Budget Forecast'!C47
36	Machine maintenance (Factory)	='Budget Forecast'!B48	='Budget Forecast'!C48
37	Salaries (Widget production)	='Budget Forecast'!B49	='Budget Forecast'!C49
38	Vehicle maintenance (Delivery)	='Budget Forecast'!B50	='Budget Forecast'!C50
39	(Spare)	='Budget Forecast'!B51	='Budget Forecast'!C51
40	Total (D)	=SUM(B34:B39)	=SUM(C34:C39)

Figure 6.5 Cash forecast formula display

42	Cash Out - Overheads		
43	Building maintenance	='Budget Forecast'!B55	='Budget Forecast'!C55
44	Machine maintenance (Office)	='Budget Forecast'!B56	='Budget Forecast'!C56
45	Petrol (Manager's cars)	='Budget Forecast'!B57	='Budget Forecast'!C57
46	Postage	='Budget Forecast'!B58	='Budget Forecast'!C58
47	Rates	='Budget Forecast'!B59	='Budget Forecast'!C59
48	Salaries (Management)	='Budget Forecast'!B60	='Budget Forecast'!C60
49	Stationery	='Budget Forecast'!B61	='Budget Forecast'!C61
50	Telephone	='Budget Forecast'!B62	='Budget Forecast'!C62
51	Vehicle maintenance (Managers)	='Budget Forecast'!B63	='Budget Forecast'!C63
52	(Spare)	='Budget Forecast'!B64	='Budget Forecast'!C64
53	Total (E)	=SUM(B43:B52)	=SUM(C43:C52)
54			
55	**Total Cash Out**		
56	(A+B+C+D+E)		
57	Total Cash Out (F)	=B18+B23+B31+B40+B53	=C18+C23+C31+C40+C53
58			
59	**Cash Flow and Bank**		
60			
61	Net cash flow	=B12-B57	=C12-C57
62			
63	Balance B/F Enter figure >>	35000	=B66
64	Cash In	=B12	=C12
65	Cash Out	=B57	=C57
66	Balance C/F	=B63+B64-B65	=C63+C64-C65
67		=IF(B66=$B$70,"Min","")	=IF(C66=$B$70,"Min","")

Figure 6.5 Continued

Again, as for the budget forecast error detecting check sums are best included.

● For example, the ranges and names given to them in the downloaded illustration framework are:

Cost category block	Range	Name of created range
CASH IN	B9:M11	CASHIN
CAPITAL	B15:M17	CASHCAPITAL
START UP COSTS	B21:M22	CASHSTARTUP
VARIABLE DIRECT COSTS	B26:M30	CASHVARIABLE
CONSTANT DIRECT COSTS	B34:M39	CASHCONSTANT
OVERHEADS	B43:M52	CASHOVERHEAD

● Enter a SUM formulae for each of the ranges, in column P, as follows:

In cell	Enter
P12	=SUM(CASHIN)
P18	=SUM(CASHCAPITAL)
P23	=SUM(CASHSTARTUP)
P31	=SUM(CASHVARIABLE)
P40	=SUM(CASHCONSTANT)
P53	=SUM(CASHOVERHEAD)

- To check that all of the formulae are correct, I have created another named range CASHOUT for P18:P53. In P61 I have put **=SUM(CASHIN)-SUM(CASHOUT)** which subtracts the total cash out from the total cash in, which should be the same as the net cash flow for the year in N61.

- I have put a comparison of P61 and N61 in A4 as

  =IF(TRUNC(N61)<>TRUNC(P61),"!!!! CHECK SUM ERROR !!!!","")

- A4 will be blank if everything adds up properly or will display the message "!!!! CHECK SUM ERROR !!!!" if not.

Notes on the cash forecast

1 CASH IN – SALES

We'll assume that cash in from sales is received one month after the sale shown in the sales forecast, which means that we needed a 'one month later' offset. Thus February in the cash forecast is linked to January in the budget forecast.

Because in the illustration there isn't a forecast for the previous year, no *cash* in for January is available from the budget.

2 CASH OUT – CAPITAL

For capital we will assume that cash is paid out in the same month as shown in the budget. Thus January in the cash forecast is linked to January in the budget forecast, February to February and so on.

3 CASH OUT – START UP

For start up we will assume that cash is paid out in the same month as shown in the budget. Thus January in the cash forecast is linked to January in the budget forecast, February to February and so on.

4 CASH OUT – VARIABLE DIRECT

The offsets for variable direct costs are very much dependent upon their nature, and quite probably somewhat variable according to pre-vailing circumstances.

- **Parts for widgets** We'll assume that parts are ordered and received one month before they are converted into finished widgets, and that it is another month before the widgets are sold. So parts are received *two months before* the widget appears in the sales forecast. The supplier invoices immediately on delivery to us, but allows 30 days for payment; so the cash is paid out for them one month later, which is one month before they appear in the sales forecast. A table might help!

Table 6.1 Paying for widget parts

	Jan	Feb	Mar
Part ordered and received	XX		
Purchase invoice sent (30 days)	XX		
Parts used in manufacture		XX	
Widget sales			XX
Parts paid for		XX	

Now, the cost of widget parts is calculated in the budget forecast, so we need to link the cash flow forecast to the budget forecast using an offset of *one month before*. So January in the cash forecast is linked to February in the budget forecast. These links are copied as far as *November*. We can't include December in the linking because that will refer to widget sales in January of the following year.

- **Diesel fuel (Deliveries)** Diesel fuel for deliveries is bought in the same month as widgets are sold, and we'll assume that we receive 30 days' credit on its purchase. That means we pay for fuel one month after the sale, and thus the first payment in this forecast will not appear until February. Link February in the cash forecast to January in the budget forecast and copy to the end of the year.

- **Wages (Temporary staff)** Wages are paid weekly, and the cost of them is incurred in line with sales. Remember that these are temporary staff, taken on for packing and distribution of completed widgets. Strictly speaking, then, there should be a one-week offset *after* sales. But the model is built on a monthly basis, so a one-week offset is not easily incorporated. If we assume that wages are paid in the same month as sales, we'll be right for three weeks of a four-week month, and that will be accurate enough for our purpose.

5   CASH OUT – CONSTANT DIRECT

For constant directs we'll assume that cash is paid out in the same month as they are shown in the budget.

6   CASH OUT – OVERHEADS

For overheads we'll assume that cash is paid out for all of them in the same month as they are shown in the budget. But bear in mind that any individual row, of any category, can be set for any other offset that may be appropriate.

7   CASH FLOW AND BANK

This block uses only spreadsheet links, that is, the references are to cells within the cash flow forecast as shown in Figure 6.4 (earlier).

- **Net cash flow** This is simply Cash In *minus* Cash Out.

- **Balance B/F** Balance brought forward is the previous month's balance carried forward. Because there is no forecast for the previous year, there is no balance brought forward in January and the first entry is therefore in February.

- **Cash In and Cash Out** These are repeats of 'Total Cash In' and 'Total Cash Out' for the sake of clarity.

- **Balance C/F** The balance is calculated by adding 'Cash In' to 'Balance B/F' and subtracting 'Cash Out'.

And that completes work on the cash flow forecast. Because it draws all of its data from the *budget forecast*, nothing more will need to be added, except for some dummy figures that will be put into the cells that are empty because there are no forecasts for the previous or following years.

	A	B	C	N	O	P
1	File name :	Chapter 6 Illustration Framework.xls				
2	Version:	1				
3	Current date and time:					
4						
5	Click here to jump the charts			Year		Check
6		Jan	Feb	Total		Sums
7						
8	**Cash In**					
9	From sales - Widgets Mk1		2,500	**27,500**		
10	From sales - Widgets Mk2		1,750	**19,250**		
11	(Spare)		0	**0**		
12	Total Cash In	0	4,250	**46,750**		46,750
13						
14	**Cash out - Capital**					
15	Factory machinery	0	0	**15,000**		
16	Office machinery	0	0	**30,000**		
17	(Spare)	0	0	**0**		
18	Total (A)	0	0	**45,000**		45,000
19						
20	**Cash Out - Startup**					
21	Design of Widget Mk3	0	0	**0**		
22	(Spare)	0	0	**0**		
23	Total (B)	0	0	**0**		0
24						
25	**Cash Out - Variable Direct**					
26	Parts for Widgets Mk1	500	500	**6,000**		
27	Parts for Widgets Mk2	300	300	**3,600**		
28	Diesel fuel (Deliveries)	0	0	**0**		
29	Wages (Temporary staff)	0	0	**0**		
30	(Spare)			**0**		
31	Total (C)	800	800	**9,600**		9,600
32						
33	**Cash Out - Constant Direct**					
34	Electricity	0	0	**0**		
35	Gas	0	0	**0**		
36	Machine maintenance (Factory)	0	0	**0**		
37	Salaries (Widget production)	0	0	**0**		
38	Vehicle maintenance (Delivery)	0	0	**0**		
39	(Spare)	0	0	**0**		
40	Total (D)	0	0	**0**		0

Figure 6.6 Cash forecast normal display, columns D–M hidden

41					
42	**Cash Out - Overheads**				
43	Building maintenance	0	0	**0**	
44	Machine maintenance (Office)	0	0	**0**	
45	Petrol (Manager's cars)	0	0	**0**	
46	Postage	0	0	**0**	
47	Rates	0	0	**0**	
48	Salaries (Management)	0	0	**0**	
49	Stationery	0	0	**0**	
50	Telephone	0	0	**0**	
51	Vehicle maintenance (Manager	0	0	**0**	
52	(Spare)	0	0	**0**	
53	Total (E)	0	0	**0**	0
54					
55	**Total Cash Out**				
56	**(A+B+C+D+E)**				
57	Total Cash Out (F)	800	800	**54,600**	54,600
58					
59	**Cash Flow and Bank**				
60					
61	Net cash flow	-800	3,450	**-7,850**	-7,850
62					
63	Balance B/F Enter figure >>	35,000	34,200	**380,950**	
64	Cash In	0	4,250	**46,750**	
65	Cash Out	800	800	**54,600**	
66	Balance C/F	34,200	37,650		

Figure 6.6 Continued

Finally, you might find a summary of the offsets used in the cash flow useful. The arrows point to the source column (month) in either the sales or budget forecasts: an up arrow ↑ indicates that the link is to the same month.

		Jan	Feb
	CASH IN		
7	From sales – Widgets MK	◄————————O	
8	From sales – Widgets Mk2	◄————————O	
11	--		
12	CASH OUT – CAPITAL		
13	Factory machinery	↑	↑
14	Office machinery	↑	↑
17	--		
18	CASH OUT – START UP		
19	Design of Widget Mk3	↑	↑
22	--		
23	CASH OUT – VARIABLE DIRECT		
24	Parts for Widgets Mk1	O————————►	
25	Parts for Widgets Mk2	O————————►	
26	Diesel fuel (Deliveries)	◄————————O	
27	Wages (Temporary staff)	↑	↑
30	--		
31	CASH OUT – CONSTANT DIRECT		
32	Electricity	↑	↑
33	Gas	↑	↑
34	Machine maintenance (Factory)	↑	↑
35	Salaries (Widget production)	↑	↑
36	Vehicle maintenance (Delivery)	↑	↑
39	--		
40	CASH OUT – OVERHEADS		
41	Building maintenance	↑	↑
42	Machine maintenance (Office)	↑	↑
43	Petrol (Manager's cars)	↑	↑
44	Postage	↑	↑
45	Rates	↑	↑
46	Salaries (Management)	↑	↑
47	Stationery	↑	↑
48	Telephone	↑	↑
49	Vehicle maintenance (Managers)	↑	↑

Figure 6.7 Cash flow offsets

Summary

In this chapter we have:

- created a sales forecast framework;

- and a budget forecast framework, with links back to the sales forecast to enable automatic update of revenue and variable direct costs when the sales forecast is altered;

- and a cash flow forecast framework with links to the end budget forecast: it required no additional data entry, except for dummy figures for the bank 'Balance B/F' and other cells that normally rely on the existence of forecasts for the previous and following years.

PART 4

Using the
illustration
framework

The illustration frameworks are now ready for use. In Part 4 we'll deal with the financial aspects of making the forecasts, and the reiterative process of fine tuning them. We'll also look at subsequential departmental budget allocations.

We'll discuss the ways in which forecasts can be reviewed using actual performance data, together with the review implications for the remainder of the forecast year. Key ratios, which are shorthand means of monitoring performance, are introduced and incorporated in the forecast.

Profitability of both the whole company, and of individual products, is always of interest and we'll use charts as necessary to help us.

Note: All monetary figures exclude Value Added Tax unless explicitly stated otherwise.

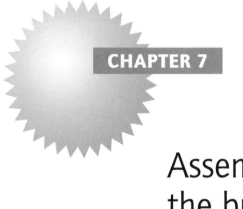

CHAPTER 7

Assembling
the budget

This chapter is about ...

Completing the sales and budget forecasts for the illustration framework, setting necessary cash flow forecast adjustments, and adding charts, key indicators and ratios.

> **Note:** All of the steps in this chapter have been completed in the downloaded spreadsheet Completed Illustration Framework.xls.
>
> If you want to create Completed Illustration Framework.xls for yourself, make a copy of Chapter 6 Illustration Framework.xls, rename it as Completed Illustration Framework.xls and follow the steps in this chapter.

Making the sales forecast

In the case of Widget Makers Ltd there are only two products to consider – Widgets Mk1 and Widgets Mk2. All that is needed are entries for each product in each month of the sales forecast's span: one year.

Entering the figures only takes a few minutes of course but what is more important is the experience and expertise of the company's managers and salesforce, and the many factors that they have to take into account.

Spreadsheet forecasts and budgets enable us to instantly test the financial impact of any sales profile that may be imagined. And this can have the most profound effect on the way in which forecasting is carried out and sales targets are set. For instance, the individual and overall impact on profitability of various product sales volumes can be quickly tested, and this may result in a radically different sales policy and strategy compared with that based on minimal testing, or indeed wholly gut feeling.

All of this suggests that the forecasting process is one of reiteration, rather than a single run through from start to finish, and in fact, that is the case throughout. When we look at monitoring and reviewing later on we will see that these are also a process of reiteration.

brilliant tip

Monitoring, comparing, reviewing and reforecasting are the essential and most prominent features of budget forecasts. It is worth repeating the truism that 'there is only one certainty in a forecast – it is wronq', and all concerned need to continually compare it with actual performance and refine it for the best possible accuracy.

The figures that we are about to enter should thus be considered a first stab at the forecast: it will almost certainly be modified several times once the rest of the budget is finalised and its effect seen.

Let's assume that at least all of the following have been taken into account in deciding the first shot at the sales volumes for the year:

- economic factors;
- factors affecting the industry sector;
- seasonal factors;
- the company's growth policy;
- capital investment plans;
- marketing strategy plans;
- production capability;
- financing arrangements;
- market sector competition.

And having considered them, we decide to first of all see how a flat profile will look, based on the average sales for each product for the previous year:

Average sales/month – Widgets Mk1: 200

Average sales/month – Widgets Mk2: 100.

The pricing policy must also be decided; should we increase, decrease or maintain the previous year's prices. Many of the sales volume factors above will also have a bearing on the pricing decision, and as for sales volumes, the process of reiteration will be used before finalising it.

Let's assume that Widgets Mk1 is the longer established of the two products, has less facility than Widgets Mk2, and is cheaper to produce. The selling price for the first run through the budget will be:

Sales price per unit of Widgets Mk1 : £275.00

Sales price per unit of Widgets Mk2 : £400.00.

These figures can now be entered on the Sales Forecast tab of the spreadsheet and the completed sales forecast is shown in Figure 7.1.

	A	B	C	D	E	F	G
1	File name :	Completed Illustration Framework.xls					Widget
2	Version:	1					Sal
3	Current date and time:						
4							
5		Jan	Feb	Mar	Apr	May	Jun
6	*** SALES ***						
7	Volume						
8	Widgets Mk1	200	200	200	200	200	200
9	Widgets Mk2	100	100	100	100	100	100
10	(Spare)						
11	Total Volume	300	300	300	300	300	300
12							
13	Price per unit (£)						
14	Widgets Mk1	275	275	275	275	275	275
15	Widgets Mk2	400	400	400	400	400	400
16							
17	Sales Value (£)						
18	Widgets Mk1	55,000	55,000	55,000	55,000	55,000	55,000
19	Widgets Mk2	40,000	40,000	40,000	40,000	40,000	40,000
20	(Spare)						
21	Total Value	95,000	95,000	95,000	95,000	95,000	95,000

Figure 7.1 The completed sales forecast (Jan–June)

Right, that's the sales forecast done; now we'll move on to the budget.

Making the budget forecast

Bearing in mind that the process of making a budget is one of reiteration, should all of the costs be put in at this stage, or only those that affect trading profitability, and then add non-trading expenditure like capital and start up later? It really doesn't matter at all, because it's so easy to change things around, add and remove costs or alter prices and volumes as much as you want.

For Widget Makers Ltd we'll put everything in to start with, and see how the budget and cash flow look before considering changes. Figure 7.2 shows the budget spreadsheet after entry of all of the figures.

It doesn't matter in what order cost decisions and entries into the spreadsheet are made, but we'll take them as they appear on the budget forecast model, in cost category order.

The detail of the entries given for each heading below are repeated in a summary for the whole budget at the end of the section.

Capital costs

These are items of expenditure that have a realisable value – they are *assets* of the company.

Factory machinery

A new widget manufacturing machine will be bought in March at a cost of £50,000. The new machine will enable widget production volumes to increase without the need for additional production staff once it has been brought into service in September. Until then, monthly production volumes cannot increase more than 10 per cent above those in January at the start of the year. Enter:

Row	Heading	Month(s)	£
19	Factory machinery	Mar	50,000

Office machinery

A replacement photocopier is needed, and will be bought in May at a cost of £5,000. In October a new computer system will be installed that will enable administration costs to be contained in the following years as the business grows. Enter:

Row	Heading	Month(s)	£
20	Office machinery	May	5,000
20	Office machinery	Oct	25,000

Start up costs

These are 'one-off' items of expenditure incurred solely through the development or introduction of a new product.

Design of Widget Mk3

In this case a new widget, the Mk3, is being developed. There is an initial cost of £10,000 for engineering design consultancy in April, then a monthly design development cost of £2,000 for the remainder of the year. Enter:

Row	Heading	Month(s)	£
25	Design of Widget Mk3	Apr	10,000
25	Design of Widget Mk3	May–Dec	2,000

Variable direct costs/item

These are the costs per widget, which are multiplied by the widget volumes, to generate the variable direct costs. Remember that you put the formulae that carry out this calculation into the spreadsheet in Chapter 6.

Parts for widgets

For now, you can assume a constant cost of parts throughout the year, although it's possible that a change may have to be made later on. The cost of parts for Widgets Mk2 are higher than those for Mk1. Enter:

Row	Heading	Month(s)	£
30	Parts for Widgets Mk1	Jan–Dec	140
31	Parts for Widgets Mk2	Jan–Dec	160

Diesel fuel (Deliveries)

This is the fuel used by the vehicles delivering widgets to customers. In a new business the cost per widget would at this stage be an estimate, but in an established business you can easily derive the figure by dividing the previous year's total cost of diesel fuel by the number of widgets delivered during that year. Remember this is per widget.

	A	B	C	D	E	F	G	H	I	J	K	L	M	N	O	P
1	FILE:	Completed Illustration Framework.xls														
2	Version:	1														
3	Cash Flow Forecast:	<DATE>	<TIME>				Widget Makers Ltd									
4							Budget Forecast									
5																
6		Jan	Feb	Mar	Apr	May	Jun	Jul	Aug	Sep	Oct	Nov	Dec	Year Total		Check Sums
7	**Sales**															
8	Volume – Widgets Mk1	200	200	200	200	200	200	200	200	200	200	200	200	2,400		
9	Volume – Widgets Mk2	100	100	100	100	100	100	100	100	100	100	100	100	1,200		
10	(Spare)															
11	Total volume	300	300	300	300	300	300	300	300	300	300	300	300	3,600		
12																
13	Value – Widgets Mk1	55,000	55,000	55,000	55,000	55,000	55,000	55,000	55,000	55,000	55,000	55,000	55,000	660,000		
14	Value – Widgets Mk2	40,000	40,000	40,000	40,000	40,000	40,000	40,000	40,000	40,000	40,000	40,000	40,000	480,000		
15	(Spare)															
16	Total £ Value	95,000	95,000	95,000	95,000	95,000	95,000	95,000	95,000	95,000	95,000	95,000	95,000	1,140,000		
17																
18	**Capital costs**															
19	Factory machinery			50,000										50,000		
20	Office machinery					5,000					25,000			30,000		
21	(Spare)															
22	Total (A)	0	0	50,000	0	5,000	0	0	0	0	25,000	0	0	80,000		80,000
23																
24	**Start up costs**															
25	Design of Widget Mk3				10,000	2,000	2,000	2,000	2,000	2,000	2,000	2,000	2,000	26,000		
26	(Spare)															
27	Total (B)	0	0	0	10,000	2,000	2,000	2,000	2,000	2,000	2,000	2,000	2,000	26,000		26,000
28																
29	**Variable Direct Costs/Item**															
30	Parts for Widgets Mk1	140	140	140	140	140	140	140	140	140	140	140	140			
31	Parts for Widgets Mk2	160	160	160	160	160	160	160	160	160	160	160	160			
32	Diesel fuel (Deliveries)	8	8	8	8	8	8	8	8	8	8	8	8			
33	Wages (Temporary staff)	15	15	15	15	15	15	15	15	15	15	15	15			
34	(Spare)															
35																

	A	B	C	D	E	F	G	H	I	J	K	L	M	N	O	P
36	**Variable Direct Costs**															
37	(Vol x Cost / Item)															
38	Parts for Widgets Mk1	28,000	28,000	28,000	28,000	28,000	28,000	28,000	28,000	28,000	28,000	28,000	28,000	336,000		
39	Parts for Widgets Mk2	16,000	16,000	16,000	16,000	16,000	16,000	16,000	16,000	16,000	16,000	16,000	16,000	192,000		
40	Diesel fuel (Deliveries)	2,400	2,400	2,400	2,400	2,400	2,400	2,400	2,400	2,400	2,400	2,400	2,400	28,800		
41	Wages (Temporary staff)	4,500	4,500	4,500	4,500	4,500	4,500	4,500	4,500	4,500	4,500	4,500	4,500	54,000		
42	(Spare)													0		
43	Total (C)	50,900	50,900	50,900	50,900	50,900	50,900	50,900	50,900	50,900	50,900	50,900	50,900			610,800
44																
45	**Constant Direct Costs**															
46	Electricity		500			500			500			500		2,000		
47	Gas			900			700			200			700	2,500		
48	Machine maintenance (Factory)	600	600	600	600	600	600	600	600	600	600	600	600	7,200		
49	Salaries (Widget production)	20,000	20,000	20,000	20,000	20,000	20,000	20,000	20,000	20,000	20,000	20,000	20,000	240,000		
50	Vehicle maintenance (Delivery)	300	300	300	300	300	300	300	300	300	300	300	300	3,600		
51	(Spare)													0		
52	Total (D)	20,900	21,400	21,800	20,900	21,400	21,600	20,900	21,400	21,100	20,900	21,400	21,600			255,300
53																
54	**Overheads**															
55	Building maintenance	400	400	400	400	2,900	400	400	400	400	400	400	400	7,300		
56	Machine maintenance (Office)	100	100	100	100	100	100	100	100	100	100	100	100	1,200		
57	Petrol (Manager's cars)	600	600	600	600	600	600	600	600	600	600	600	600	7,200		
58	Postage	90	90	90	90	90	90	90	90	90	90	90	90	1,080		
59	Rates	200			200	200	200	200	200	200	200	200	200	2,000		
60	Salaries (Management)	17,000	17,000	17,000	17,000	17,000	17,000	17,000	17,000	17,000	17,000	17,000	17,000	204,000		
61	Stationery	85	85	85	85	85	85	85	85	85	85	85	85	1,020		
62	Telephone		325			325			325			325		1,300		
63	Vehicle maintenance (Managers)	100	100	100	100	100	100	100	100	100	100	100	100	1,200		
64	(Spare)													0		
65	Total (E)	18,575	18,700	18,375	18,575	21,400	18,575	18,575	18,900	18,575	18,575	18,900	18,575			226,300
66																
67	**Total Costs**															
68	(A+B+C+D+E)															
69	Total (F)	90,375	91,000	141,075	100,375	100,700	93,075	92,375	93,200	92,575	117,375	93,200	93,075			1,198,400
70																

Figure 7.2 The completed budget forecast

Enter:

Row	Heading	Month(s)	£
32	Diesel fuel (Deliveries)	Jan–Dec	8

Wages (Temporary staff)

These wages are for temporary staff taken on as and when required to assist with widget packing and delivery. Again, for a new business the figure per widget will be an estimate, or in an established business, calculated by dividing the previous year's total cost of temporary staff's wages by the widget volumes for that year. Remember this is per widget.

Enter:

Row	Heading	Month(s)	£
33	Wages (Temporary staff)	Jan–Dec	15

Constant direct costs

These are the costs directly associated with the products, but not immediately affected by normal fluctuations in volume.

Electricity

This is used for lighting and machinery operation. Although the amount used is somewhat dependent upon production volumes, the swing is not that significant, and a value based on the annual production volumes is good enough for the purpose of the budget. Enter:

Row	Heading	Month(s)	£
46	Electricity	Feb	500
46	Electricity	May	500
46	Electricity	Aug	500
46	Electricity	Nov	500

Note: It would be normal to show utility costs as an average amount for each month, especially where there is no significant seasonal variation, i.e. £2,000/12. But showing them quarterly here is useful for illustrative purposes.

Gas

Used predominantly for factory heating, the quarterly bills reflect seasonal requirements. Enter:

Row	Heading	Month(s)	£
47	Gas	Mar	900
47	Gas	Jun	700
47	Gas	Sep	200
47	Gas	Dec	700

Note: Again it would be normal to show utility costs as an average amount for each month, in this case using a third of each quarter's figure per month, but showing them quarterly here is useful for illustrative purposes.

Machine maintenance (Factory)

The factory machines are routinely maintained under a contract covering both parts and labour. The contract terms require a monthly payment. Enter:

Row	Heading	Month(s)	£
48	Machine mt'ce (Factory)	Jan–Dec	600

Salaries (Widget production)

These are the salaries of all full-time staff directly involved in widget production. Enter:

Row	Heading	Month(s)	£
49	Salaries (Widget production)	Jan–Dec	20,000

Vehicle maintenance (Delivery)

Although regular mileage services can be forecast to specific months, there are also irregular breakdowns to allow for. One way of handling any expense where the value can be anticipated, but the 'when' is unknown, is to derive an annual figure and spread it evenly through the year. Then, each month when actual expenditure is monitored, you can either move forward any 'unused' portion of the figure to the next month, or once again spread it over what remains of the year. Using this method, enter:

Row	Heading	Month(s)	£
50	Vehicle mt'ce (Delivery)	Jan–Dec	300

Overhead costs

These are all trading costs not directly related to a product, and which are also neither capital nor start up.

Building maintenance

This consists principally of factory and office cleaning which is invoiced monthly but, in addition, external painting will be carried out in the early summer. Enter:

Row	Heading	Month(s)	£
55	Building maintenance	Jan–Apr	400
55	Building maintenance	Jun–Dec	400
55	Building maintenance	May	2,900

brilliant tip

Put the May figures in as **=400+2500** to act as a reminder that there are two components to the cost.

Machine maintenance (Office)

Photocopiers, computers and fax machines are all maintained under a maintenance contract that covers parts and labour for a monthly premium. Enter:

Row	Heading	Month(s)	£
56	Machine maintenance (Office)	Jan–Dec	100

Petrol (Managers' cars)

Although there will obviously be fluctuations in this expense from month to month, they are very difficult to predict, and in any case are small compared with the total overheads. An annual spread of the year's total forecast expenditure on petrol is, therefore, fine. Enter:

Row	Heading	Month(s)	£
57	Petrol (Managers' cars)	Jan–Dec	600

Postage

Like most other general administration costs, fluctuations in monthly costs are comparatively inconsequential and the year's forecast total may be spread throughout the year. Enter:

Row	Heading	Month(s)	£
58	Postage	Jan–Dec	90

Rates

Business rates are usually paid monthly for 10 months of the year, from April to January inclusive. Enter:

Row	Heading	Month(s)	£
59	Rates	Jan	200
59	Rates	Apr–Dec	200

Note: It would be normal to show rates as an average amount for each month, but showing them over 10 months is useful for cash forecasting purposes.

Salaries (Management)

These are the salaries of managers and staff not directly involved in production. They include all additional costs such as National Insurance and pension contributions, although you may want to separately identify those components, as would also be the case for other extras such as bonus and productivity payments. Enter:

Row	Heading	Month(s)	£
60	Salaries (Management)	Jan–Dec	17,000

Stationery

For the same reasons as for postage, an even spread of the forecast annual cost is fine. Enter:

Row	Heading	Month(s)	£
61	Stationery	Jan–Dec	85

Telephone

The telephone bill is paid quarterly, and although there are minor seasonal fluctuations, the year's forecast split equally into four payments is fine for our needs. Enter:

Row	Heading	Month(s)	£
62	Telephone	Feb	325
62	Telephone	May	325
62	Telephone	Aug	325
62	Telephone	Nov	325

Note: It would be normal to show telephone and similar costs as an average amount for each month, but showing them here quarterly is useful for illustrative purposes.

Vehicle maintenance (Managers)

In exactly the same way as for the delivery vehicle maintenance, an estimate of the total annual cost spread throughout the year is fine, so long as any unsent 'allocation' is rolled on from month to month. Enter:

Row	Heading	Month(s)	£
63	Vehicle mt'ce (Managers)	Jan–Dec	100

And that completes the data entry for the budget forecast. A summary table of all of them can be found in Table 7.1.

Cash flow forecast adjustments

The cash flow forecast is fully automatic in the sense that all of its data is drawn from the budget forecast. But because in the example there are no forecasts for the previous or following year, and because of the offsets that have been built into it, there are some gaps in the cash flow for January and December.

This can of course also happen in real forecasts; when, for instance, the first computer-based forecast is constructed, there will be no figures for the previous year. We need a way to deal with that situation, so that we maintain a forecast close to reality, without having to continually check and intervene.

Table 7.1 Summary of all budget data entries

Row	Heading	Month(s)	£
19	Factory machinery	Mar	50,000
20	Office machinery	May	5,000
20	Office machinery	Oct	25,000
25	Design of Widget Mk3	Apr	10,000
25	Design of Widget Mk3	May–Dec	2,000
30	Parts for Widgets Mk1	Jan–Dec	140
31	Parts for Widgets Mk2	Jan–Dec	160
32	Diesel fuel (Deliveries)	Jan–Dec	8
33	Wages (Temporary staff)	Jan–Dec	15
46	Electricity	Feb	500
46	Electricity	May	500
46	Electricity	Aug	500
46	Electricity	Nov	500
47	Gas	Mar	900
47	Gas	Jun	700
47	Gas	Sep	200
47	Gas	Dec	700
48	Machine mt'ce (Factory)	Jan–Dec	600
49	Salaries (Widget production)	Jan–Dec	20,000
50	Vehicle mt'ce (Delivery)	Jan–Dec	300
55	Building maintenance	Jan–Apr	400
55	Building maintenance	Jun–Dec	400
55	Building maintenance	May	2,900
56	Machine maintenance (Office)	Jan–Dec	100
57	Petrol (Managers' cars)	Jan–Dec	600
58	Postage	Jan–Dec	90
59	Rates	Jan	200
59	Rates	Apr–Dec	200
60	Salaries (Management)	Jan–Dec	17,000
61	Stationery	Jan–Dec	85
62	Telephone	Feb	325
62	Telephone	May	325
62	Telephone	Aug	325
62	Telephone	Nov	325
63	Vehicle mt'ce (Managers)	Jan–Dec	100

A simple solution is to pick up the figures in the adjacent month, so that when they are changed during the reiterative process of forecasting, the dummy figures will also change. We might have to modify this principle if significant differences in adjacent months are expected for the heading in question. In the case of Widget Makers Ltd, the adjacent month method will work well enough for illustrative purposes.

The gaps, as the cash flow forecast currently stands, are:

Row	Heading	Jan	Dec
9	From sales – Widgets Mk1	XX	
10	From sales – Widgets Mk2	XX	
26	Parts for Widgets Mk1		XX
27	Parts for Widgets Mk2		XX
28	Diesel fuel (Deliveries)	XX	
63	Balance B/F	XX	

With the exception of the bank Balance B/F, which I've just invented for illustrative purposes, we need to link the others to their adjacent months. So, put these links and Balance B/F figure into the cash forecast:

Row	Heading	Jan	Dec
9	From sales – Widgets Mk1	=C9	
10	From sales – Widgets Mk2	=C10	
26	Parts for Widgets Mk1		L26
27	Parts for Widgets Mk2		L27
28	Diesel fuel (Deliveries)	C28	
63	Balance B/F	35000	

Figure 7.3 (pages 162–3) shows how the cash flow forecast looks now.

Charts and key indicators

One of the more obvious features of the complete budget layout in Figure 7.2, and the cash flow layout in Figure 7.3, is that they both have a lot of numbers! You'll find that you have to study them for quite a while – especially the cash flow – to get an understanding of what's going on. More significantly, once changes start to be made, and different scenarios are being tested, it really isn't possible to absorb all of the relevant effects that are necessary for an overall view.

We have two main ways of overcoming this difficulty, *charts* and *key indicators*. With both of them, most advantage is obtained by minimising the amount of information presented, and ensuring that it is strictly appropriate to the view you are after. Both methods are extremely quick and easy to set up, and while there are a number of 'standard' charts and key indicators that you'll want to retain in your spreadsheet, others will only be set up temporarily for a specific purpose. These you can discard once the job is done.

brilliant definition

A *key indicator* is simply highlighting a feature of special interest. For example, when considering a plan for capital investment you may have to determine its effect on cash flow for a variety of proposals: will borrowing be necessary, if so, how much and when?

To see key indicators on the cash flow, scan along the closing balance row and find the lowest figure for each proposal. Have a quick look for the minimum balance on Figure 7.3.

A 'minimum balance' key indicator makes it much easier to immediately see the effect of different proposals. Here are examples of two ways of providing them:

1 In B70, use the MINimum function like this:

=MIN(B66.M66)

2 In row 67, column B, use this function:

=IF(B66=$B$70),"Min","")

and copy to December. This will compare the minimum value obtained above with each month's closing balance, and display **Min** where they are the same.

	A	B	C	D	E	F	G	H	I	J	K	L	M	N	O	P
1	FILE:	Completed Illustration Framework.xls														
2	Version:	1														
3	Current datr and time:	<DATE>	<TIME>													
4																
5						Widget Makers Ltd										
6						Cash Forecast										
		Jan	Feb	Mar	Apr	May	Jun	Jul	Aug	Sep	Oct	Nov	Dec	Year Total		Check Sums
8	**Cash in**															
9	From sales – Widgets Mk1	55,000	55,000	55,000	55,000	55,000	55,000	55,000	55,000	55,000	55,000	55,000	55,000	660,000		
10	From sales – Widgets Mk2	40,000	40,000	40,000	40,000	40,000	40,000	40,000	40,000	40,000	40,000	40,000	40,000	480,000		
11	(Spare)	0	0	0	0	0	0	0	0	0	0	0	0	0		
12	Total Cash in	95,000	95,000	95,000	95,000	95,000	95,000	95,000	95,000	95,000	95,000	95,000	95,000	1,140,000		1,140,000
13																
14	**Cash out – Captial**															
15	Factory machinery	0	0	50,000	0	0	0	0	0	0	0	0	0	50,000		
16	Office machinery	0	0	0	0	5,000	0	0	0	0	25,000	0	0	30,000		
17	(Spare)	0	0	0	0	0	0	0	0	0	0	0	0	0		
18	Total (A)	0	0	50,000	0	5,000	0	0	0	0	25,000	0	0	80,000		80,000
19																
20	**Cash out – Startup**															
21	Design of Widget Mk3	0	0	0	10,000	2,000	2,000	2,000	2,000	2,000	2,000	2,000	2,000	26,000		
22	(Spare)	0	0	0	0	0	0	0	0	0	0	0	0	0		
23	Total (B)	0	0	0	10,000	2,000	2,000	2,000	2,000	2,000	2,000	2,000	2,000	26,000		26,000
24																
25	**Cash out – Variable Direct**															
26	Parts for Widgets Mk1	28,000	28,000	28,000	28,000	28,000	28,000	28,000	28,000	28,000	28,000	28,000	28,000	336,000		
27	Parts for Widgets Mk2	16,000	16,000	16,000	16,000	16,000	16,000	16,000	16,000	16,300	16,000	16,000	16,000	192,000		
28	Diesel fuel (Deliveries)	2,400	2,400	2,400	2,400	2,400	2,400	2,400	2,400	2,400	2,400	2,400	2,400	28,800		
29	Wages (Temporary staff)	4,500	4,500	4,500	4,500	4,500	4,500	4,500	4,500	4,500	4,500	4,500	4,500	54,000		
30	(Spare)	0	0	0	0	0	0	0	0	0	0	0	0	0		
31	Total (C)	50,900	50,900	50,900	50,900	50,900	50,900	50,900	50,900	50,300	50,900	50,900	50,900	610,800		610,800
32																

	A	B	C	D	E	F	G	H	I	J	K	L	M	N	O	P
33	**Cash out – Constant direct**															
34	Electricity	0	500	0	0	500	0	0	500	0	0	500	0	2,000		
35	Gas	0	0	900	0	0	700	0	0	200	0	0	700	2,500		
36	Machine maintenance (Factory)	600	600	600	600	600	600	600	600	600	600	600	600	7,200		
37	Salaries (Widget production)	20,000	20,000	20,000	20,000	20,000	20,000	20,000	20,000	20,000	20,000	20,000	20,000	240,000		
38	Vehicle maintenance (Delivery)	300	300	300	300	300	300	300	300	300	300	300	300	3600		
39	(Spare)	0	0	0	0	0	0	0	0	0	0	0	0	0		
40	Total (D)	20,900	21,400	21,800	20,900	21,400	21,600	20,900	21,400	21,100	20,900	21,400	21,600	255,300		255,300
41																
42	**Cash out – Overheads**															
43	Building maintenance	400	400	400	400	2,900	400	400	400	400	400	400	400	7,300		
44	Machine maintenance (Office)	100	100	100	100	100	100	100	100	100	100	100	100	1,200		
45	Petrol (Manager's cars)	600	600	600	600	600	600	600	600	600	600	600	600	7,200		
46	Postage	90	90	90	90	90	90	90	90	90	90	90	90	1,080		
47	Rates	200	200	0	200	200	200	200	200	200	200	200	200	2,000		
48	Salaries (Management)	17,000	17,000	17,000	17,000	17,000	17,000	17,000	17,000	17,000	17,000	17,000	17,000	204,000		
49	Stationery	85	85	85	85	85	85	85	85	85	85	85	85	1,020		
50	Telephone	0	325	0	0	325	0	0	325	0	0	325	0	1,300		
51	Vehicle maintenance (Managers)	100	100	100	100	100	100	100	100	100	100	100	100	1,200		
52	(Spare)	0	0	0	0	0	0	0	0	0	0	0	0	0		
53	Total (E)	18,575	18,700	18,375	18,575	21,400	18,575	18,575	18,900	18,575	18,575	18,900	18,575	226,300		226,300
54																
55	**Total cash out**															
56	(A+B+C+D+E)															
57	Total Cash Out (F)	90,375	91,000	141,075	100,375	100,700	93,075	92,375	93,200	92,575	117,375	93,200	93,075	1,198,400		1,198,400
58																
59	**Cash flow and bank**															
60																
61	Net cash flow	4,625	4,000	−46,075	−5,375	−5,700	1,925	2,625	1,800	2,425	−22,375	1,800	1,925	−58,400		−58,400
62																
63	Balance B/F Enter figure >>	35,000	39,625	43,625	−2,450	−7,825	−13,525	11,600	−8,975	−7,175	−4,750	−27,125	−25,325			
64	Cash In	95,000	95,000	95,000	95,000	95,000	95,000	95,000	95,000	95,000	95,000	95,000	95,000	1,140,000		
65	Cash Out	90,375	91,000	141,075	100,375	100,700	93,075	92,375	93,200	92,575	117,375	93,200	93,075	1,198,400		
66	Balance C/F	39,625	43,625	−2,450	−7,825	−13,525	−11,600	−8,975	−7,175	−4,750	−27,125	−25,325	−23,400			
67																

Figure 7.3 The completed cash flow forecast

The result of both of these is shown in Figure 7.4, which is part of the cash forecast. The minimum balance is shown at B70 (it could of course be put anywhere on the spreadsheet), and 'Min' is displayed in row 68 below where the minimum occurs.

57	A		B	C	D		J	K	L
58									
59	CASH FLOW AND BANK		Jan	Feb	Mar		Sep	Oct	Nov
60									
61	Net cash flow		4,625	4,000	−46,075		2,425	−22,375	1,800
62									
63	Balance B/F Enter figure >>		35,000	39,625	43,625		−7,175	−4,750	−27,125
64	Cash In		95,000	95,000	95,000		95,000	95,000	95,000
65	Cash Out		90,375	91,000	141,075		92,575	117,375	93,200
66	Balance C/F		39,625	43,625	−2,450		−4,750	−27,125	−25,325
67									
68								Min	
69	KEY INDICATORS								
70	Minimum balance		−27,125						

Figure 7.4 Minimum balance key indicator

Charts are most useful for displaying trends and comparisons, but be careful not to put too much information on one chart, or it will become as difficult to interpret as rows of figures. Sometimes it's also useful to include a key indicator on a chart.

Figure 7.5, which is a chart at the bottom of the cash flow spreadsheet, shows the closing balance and net cash flow for each month graphically. It also displays the minimum closing bank balance as a figure at the top right, and the annual net cash flow at the top centre.

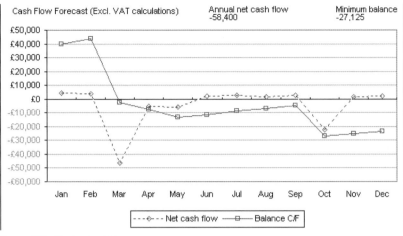

Figure 7.5 Cash chart 1

Key ratios

A *key ratio* is usually the result of one figure divided by another, but the term can be used for any arithmetic operation carried out on a number of figures to produce a single meaningful result.

For example, monthly sales can be divided by the number of people employed to give £ Sales per employee, usually written as:

£ Sales/Employee

Or net profit divided by widget sales volumes, gives:

£ Net Profit/Widget

More key ratios

Direct cost/sale
Direct costs/direct employee
Direct costs/total costs
Gross profit/employee
Gross profit/sale
Net profit/employee
Net profit/sale
Overhead cost/sale
Overhead costs/employee
Overhead costs/direct costs
Overhead costs/total costs
Sales/direct employee
Total cost/sale

Key ratios may also be presented as percentage values, for example:

- Gross profit as a percentage of sales
- Net profit as a percentage of sales.

You might find percentage values easier to relate to than the raw ratio figure.

Averages can also provide figures that will help to isolate and highlight significant features of a company's budget. They are most useful for smoothing the peaks and troughs that would otherwise obscure a clear view of performance trends. For example:

- average cash flow;
- average variable direct costs;
- average sales;
- average total cost;
- average overheads.

Charts, key indicators, key ratios, percentages and averages are the basic analytical tools of the budget forecaster's trade. But they should only be used when necessary, often for a specific task, after which you can discard them. It is very easy to create large numbers of diverse analytical figures and ratios on a spreadsheet, but if there are too many, their significance is likely to be lost; instead of clarifying the spreadsheet, it will become even harder to interpret.

Summary

In this chapter we have:

- entered the first estimates of sales and budget forecast figures into the spreadsheet models;
- looked at the rationale behind how costs have been spread;
- adjusted the cash flow forecast with 'intelligent dummy' figures to generate a meaningful view of the year;
- seen the use of charts and key indicators;
- learned that key ratios and other analytical tools and figures provide valuable insight, but only if used sparingly and with caution.

The complete illustration framework is now assembled and is ready for closer examination and any necessary adjustments – the reiteration process.

Note: The downloaded version of the completed framework is the file 'Completed Illustration Framework.xls'.

CHAPTER 8

Causes and effects

This chapter is about ...

The way in which changes in volume and timing of sales and costs can affect profitability and cash flow, and the practical aspects of testing them – such as where to start and how to use a reiteration process.

We'll alter sales, cost and timing factors making simple, single changes to more complex, multiple changes, and look at their impact on the figures and charts.

Adjustment and refinement

If figures have been put into the sales and budget forecast illustration frameworks, *and* the cash flow forecast has been linked to them *and* the forecasters and their colleagues are completely satisfied with what they show, then no further work on them is necessary and they can be put to work immediately for budget allocation and operational monitoring. But usually life isn't like that!

Budget forecasting is, more often than not, a process of adjustment and refinement, of reiteration through the models until everyone is satisfied – for now – that what they show represents the most realistic forecast of reality they can muster. And of course, this reiteration is what spread-sheet-based forecasts are so good at, partly because they recalculate changes in a flash, but more significantly because the relationships between all of the elements, the causes and effects, are intrinsically built into the models.

In this chapter we'll consider the practical aspects of reiteration, and look at simple cause and effect examples.

Notes:

1   The downloaded version of the completed framework is the file 'Completed Illustration Framework.xls.

2   There are additional features in Completed Illustration Framework.xls which we'll be looking at throughout the remainder of the book.

3   In the downloaded pack there is also a file – Original Completed Illustration Framework.xls – which you can copy to recreate Completed Illustration Framework.xls, to save setting the framework back to its original state after trying the cause and effect illustrations.

The reiteration process

In the world of sales and P&L forecasting, reiteration on the scale that we'll use was unheard of before computers. Reiteration of the budgeting process is extremely important; not only does it cut down on errors, but also provides opportunities to spot many more significant features that might otherwise be lost amongst all that data. But this highlights that we should use key indicators, ratios and graphs sparingly with only essential details.

brilliant tip

Because there are so many figures and factors to consider just focus on one or two at a time. Then change some values, see the effect and change again if necessary ... and so on. You might need to do nothing more than keep an eye on the appropriate figures or set up some key indicators, key ratios or a chart. These can be either temporary or established as permanent features. If you're not sure whether any of them will be needed again, assume that they will be, and put them in a suitable place and form. If you are certain that an indicator won't be needed again, then just put it into any convenient cell and delete it once the job is done.

Examining causes and effects

Remember that the sales, budget and cash forecasts are interlinked:

- The budget forecast picks up sales volume and sales value from the sales forecast.
- The cash forecast picks up its data from the budget forecast – except the sales figures for the charts which come direct from the sales forecast.

brilliant tip

Changes to figures must always be made at the first point in the chain. For example, change sales volume figures on the sales forecast tab, not by overwriting the formulae on the budget or cash forecast.

Note: When trying out the changes in this chapter, there is no need to restore figures to what they were, just close the spreadsheet *without saving the changes*.

Simple cause and effect

There is no better way than 'playing' with a spreadsheet model to understand the relationship between cause and effect in financial forecasts. Although the relationships can get extremely complex when many factors are involved – to the point where an average brain simply cannot cope – the spreadsheet model will still unswervingly supply the correct end result. Examples of more complex relationships will be explored in Chapter 10, but here we'll, concentrate on simple relationships – firstly by discussing a range of 'causes' and then by trying them out on the spreadsheet models for Widget Makers Ltd.

The cause factors that will be looked at are:

1 **Sales**
   - Sales volumes
   - Sales price

2 **Cost**
   - Capital expenditure
   - Start up expenditure
   - Variable direct costs
   - Constant direct costs
   - Overheads

3 **Timing**
   - Cash payment timing
   - Sales receipt timing
   - General.

There is a summary of causes and their effects at the end of this section (Figure 8.1).

1 Sales factors

Sales volumes

Does selling more mean bigger profits and a larger bank balance? Possibly, but the converse may also be true. 'Bigger profits' assumes that every item sold makes a profit, but if enough of them don't, then selling more will create a larger loss. 'Larger bank balance' also assumes profitability but, more significantly, requires a lot of qualification if there is continual sales growth. The detailed effect of volume growth on cash flow depends upon several factors, including net profit and the nature, value and timing of variable direct costs. It is quite possible for a company to run out of cash when business is booming. This subject is discussed in detail in Chapter 10.

However, if we assume profitable sales and no sales volume growth, then it's reasonable for us to assume that:

Cause		**Effect**
Higher sales volumes	$\rightarrow$	Higher gross profit
		Higher net profit
		More cash in the bank – maybe

Sales price

In any given stable situation, and ignoring any marketing and sales factors such as competition, for the purpose of budget forecasts it's safe for us to assume:

Cause		**Effect**
Higher sales price	$\rightarrow$	Higher gross profit
		Higher net profit
		More cash in the bank - maybe

2 Cost factors

Capital expenditure

There are several ways of viewing capital expenditure, and of dealing with it in a budget forecast and allocation. All we need for budget forecasting is to ensure a consistent, or at least widely understood, policy is adopted.

Some questions a forecaster needs answers to are as follows. The responses given are for Widget Makers Ltd:

(a) Is capital expenditure to be shown in the budget?*   Yes

(b) Is the expenditure a cost on gross or net profit?   No

(c) Are fixed assets to be included in the budget?   No

(d) Is depreciation of assets to be included in the budget?   No

(e) Is the interest on any capital financing to be included
      in the budget?   No

* If a cash flow will be associated with the budget, and the answer to question (b) is 'Yes', then capital expenditure must appear in both the budget and the cash flow forecasts.

If a cash flow will be associated with the budget, and the answer to question (b) is 'No', it *must* at least appear in the cash flow forecast, but may also be in both. For Widget Makers Ltd it is shown in both, although it does not figure in profitability calculations.

A final point on capital expenditure. It may well be an investment, in a new machine for instance, that will improve productivity and reduce costs. Clearly we need to account for this effect in the budget, but it isn't necessary solely for that reason to include the capital expenditure itself in the budget forecast or allocation. However, it's shown in Widget Maker's budget, but does not affect profit figures, so:

Cause		**Effect**
Capital expenditure	$\rightarrow$	Less cash in the bank

Start up expenditure

In some ways, start up expenditure begs the same questions as those for capital expenditure. If the start up cost is for a capital item, then it will be categorised and treated as such. Assuming that it isn't capital expenditure you might like to consider the following points. Again, the responses shown are those that apply to Widget Makers Ltd:

(a) Is start up expenditure to be included in the budget?*   Yes

(b) Is the expenditure a cost on gross or net profit?   No

(c) Is the interest on any start up financing to be included
    in the budget?   No

* The comments made for (b) in capital expenditure also apply to start up costs.

The points made for capital investment are also true for start up expenditure. A start up cost is often an investment in a new product, and if we have to take account of it in profitability, then it must either be regarded as an overhead, or as a direct cost of the new product even if the product doesn't yet exist.

Widget Makers Ltd have decided not to include the design and development costs in the profitability shown on the budget, although it does appear there as well as on the cash flow forecast. So:

Cause		**Effect**
Start up expenditure	$\rightarrow$	Less cash in the bank

Note: Start up costs, together with other items not included anywhere in the example budget for Widget Makers Ltd (such as loan interest and depreciation) *will* figure in profit calculations in the company's accounts. They are excluded here for the sake of simplicity.

Variable direct costs

These are costs directly associated with the product, and so directly affect gross profit, and hence also net profit.

Characteristics of *variable* direct costs that are of most interest to a forecaster include their:

- arithmetic relationship to volume;
- proportion of total (variable + constant) direct costs;
- proportion to total (direct + overhead) costs;
- timing with respect to payment for them;
- timing with respect to sales receipts;
- magnitude with respect to gross and net profit.

As can be judged by this list, variable direct costs are at the root of a number of fairly complex relationships, and we'll look at these more closely in Chapter 10. Simplistically though:

Cause		**Effect**
Higher variable direct cost	$\rightarrow$	Lower gross profit
		Lower net profit
		Less cash in the bank

The converse of these is true for lower variable direct costs.

Constant direct costs

These costs are directly associated with the product and will affect both gross and net profit.

Like all costs, the timing of payment for them is important, and in the case of constant direct costs, their proportion of both total direct costs and total overall costs. Their effects are the same as constant direct costs, but in a less dynamic way because they are not influenced by volumes:

Cause		**Effect**
Higher constant direct costs	$\rightarrow$	Lower gross profit
		Lower net profit
		Less cash in the bank

The converse of these is true for lower constant direct costs.

Overheads

These are the costs not directly associated with the products; they will therefore not affect gross profit. Their proportion of the total costs is important during volume growth, as is the timing of the payment for them on cash flow:

Cause		**Effect**
Higher overhead costs	$\rightarrow$	Lower net profit
		Less cash in the bank

The converse of these is true for lower overhead costs.

3 Timing factors

Cash payment timing

In the calculation of profit, it is *what* and *how much* that are important, whereas cash flow is all about *when* and *how much*. There is, however, a link from cash flow back to profit. If money is borrowed, whether as a formal loan, a bank overdraft, or any other kind of financing arrangement that incurs a charge, then that charge will figure in the calculation of profit. As with all other aspects of financial control, spreadsheets are ideally suited to these calculations and feeding back into the profit figures. However, interest charges have not been included in the example of Widget Makers Ltd so payment timing affects only cash flow:

Cause		**Effect**
Earlier cash payment	$\rightarrow$	Less cash in the bank
Later cash payment		More cash in the bank

Sales receipt timing

All of the points made for cash payment timing are also true for sales receipt timing, but their effects are precisely the opposite:

Cause		Effect
Earlier sales receipt	$\rightarrow$	More cash in the bank
Later sales receipt		Less cash in the bank

General

While the simple impact of cash flow timing is reflected only by the bank balance, and in the profit if interest charges are incurred, poor cash flow has much wider implications, especially during volume growth. In Chapter 10, we'll see how a fundamentally profitable business with increasing sales can run into cash availability problems. At best growth is inhibited; at worst their survival is dependent upon the consideration and forbearance of their source of finance – the bank perhaps.

Cause and effect summary

Figure 8.1 summarises simple cause and effect; ↑ means higher or better, ↓ means lower or worse. A blank entry indicates that in simple relationships there is no impact. Note that a change to *gross* profit always affects *net* profit.

CAUSES	...................EFFECTS...................			
	Gross Profit	Net Profit	Cash Flow	
Sales factors				
Sales volume higher	↑	↑	↑	
Sales volume lower	↓	↓	↑	
Sales volume increasing	↑	↑	↓	See Chapter 10
Sales volume decreasing	↓	↓	↓	See Chapter 10
Sales price up	↑	↑	↑	
Sales price down	↓	↓	↓	
Cost factors				
Capital cost	*	*	↓	*Subject to company policy
Start up cost			↓	
Variable direct cost up	↓	↓	↓	
Variable direct cost down	↑	↑	↑	
Constant direct cost up	↓	↓	↓	
Constant direct cost down	↑	↑	↑	
Overheads up		↓	↓	
Overheads down		↑	↑	
Timing factors				
Cash payment earlier			↓	
Cash payment later			↑	
Sales receipt earlier			↑	
Sales receipt later			↓	

Figure 8.1 Summary table of simple cause and effect

Address the cause or the effect?

This heading suggests that there are only two ways of deciding what changes to make in the reiterative process – looking first at the *causes* and working out the *effect* of a change, or looking first at the *effect* and working out what changes need to be made to the *causes* to achieve what we want.

There is, however, a third method – it's called 'suck it and see!' or 'trial and error'. In practice this method is probably used more than any other, and again (I know, I keep on saying it), spreadsheets are ideally suited to it. *But* it's important first to have an understanding of what's happening in the forecasts when figures are changed and the outcome checked in this way. *Then* you are properly equipped to use trial and error as much as you like.

In this section we'll look at the two formal methods with an example of each, using two of the simple cause and effects discussed earlier. Trial and error will also feature in both. These will be followed by less detailed examples of the rest of the simple cause and effects. The section will also give you practical illustrations of how to use key indicators, ratios and graphs.

Method 1

The desired *effect* is known. What changes to causes are needed?

Example 1 – Improving gross profit

In this example, calculation of gross profit is added to the budget forecast and the changes needed to improve it are examined and tested. For use later on, net profit calculations will also be added.

 brilliant definition

Gross profit = Revenue – Direct costs
Net profit = Revenue – (Direct costs + Overhead costs)

The first task is to set up some key indicators – in this case views of gross profit and net profit. A graphical representation will also be useful.

Profitability can be calculated on the budget forecast, and we're assuming that Widget Makers Ltd choose to exclude capital and start up costs from it.

The new row headings and formulae for the budget forecast in Figure 8.2 shows the calculation of gross and net profit, and how both are also expressed as percentage of sales. Only column B (Jan) is illustrated, but the formulae should be copied through to column M (Dec). The formulae in column N show how the full year's revenue and costs are used to calculate annual profit percentages.

	A	B
71		
72		
73	Profitability	
74	(Excluding capital and start up)	
75		
76	Revenue from sales	=B16
77	Direct costs – Widgets Mk 1	=B38+((B40+B41+B42)/2)+(B52/2)
78	Direct costs – Widgets Mk 2	=B39+((B40+B41+B42)/2)+(B52/2)
79	Gross profit	=B76-(B77+B78)
80	as % of sales	=B79/B76
81		
82	Overhead costs	=B65
83	Total costs	=B77+B78+B82
84	Net profit	=B76-B83
85	Net profit as % of sales	=B84/B76

Figure 8.2 Calculation of gross and net profit

Figure 8.3 shows what the profit figures look like for the forecast as it was left in the last chapter. Focus on the percentage of sales figures.

Gross profit is 24 per cent of sales, but suppose that a figure of nearer 30 per cent is wanted by December. What changes are necessary to achieve that objective?

Now then – if you *really* must, you can skip over this next bit and pick up again at 'Trial and error'. But if you do, why not try returning afterwards?

The ratio is *gross profit/sales*, and so to improve the figure, either the gross profit must be increased by a greater proportion than the sales that produce it, or sales must be reduced by a smaller proportion than their effect on gross profit. Assuming we don't want to reduce sales, we need to increase gross profit while maintaining sales at the current level.

Gross profit is revenue – direct costs, so, if sales revenue is to be held constant, direct costs must be addressed to improve gross profit.

Direct costs consist of *variable directs* and *constant directs*, and so reducing either of them will have the desired effect, but it would be best to concentrate first on the one that will have the most significant impact on total direct costs. A glance at the budget forecast shows that variable direct costs are £51,000/month, and constant direct costs are on average about £21,000/month.

A	B	C	D	E	F	G	H	I	J	K	L	M	N
73 PROFITABILITY	Jan	Feb	Mar	Apr	May	Jun	Jul	Aug	Sep	Oct	Nov	Dec	Year
74 (Excluding capital and start up)													
75													
76 Revenue from sales	95,000	95,000	95,000	95,000	95,000	95,000	95,000	95,000	95,000	95,000	95,000	95,000	1,140,000
77 Direct costs – Widgets Mk 1	41,900	42,150	42,350	41,900	42,150	42,250	41,900	42,150	42,000	41,900	42,150	42,250	505,050
78 Direct costs – Widgets Mk 2	29,900	29,830	29,716	28,959	28,908	28,713	28,073	28,040	27,612	27,240	27,223	27,062	341,277
79 Gross profit	23,200	22,700	22,300	23,200	22,700	22,500	23,200	22,700	23,000	23,200	22,700	22,500	273,900
80 Gross profit as % of sales	24.4%	24.4%	24.4%	24.4%	24.4%	24.4%	24.4%	24.4%	24.4%	24.4%	24.4%	24.4%	24.4%
81													
82 Overhead costs	18,575	18,700	18,375	18,575	21,400	18,575	18,575	18,900	18,575	18,575	18,900	18,575	226,300
83 Total costs	90,375	91,000	91,075	90,375	93,700	91,075	90,375	91,200	90,575	90,375	91,200	91,075	1,092,400
84 Net profit	4,625	4,000	3,925	4,625	1,300	3,925	4,625	3,800	4,425	4,625	3,800	3,925	47,600
85 Net profit as % of sales	4.9%	4.2%	4.1%	4.9%	1.4%	4.1%	4.9%	4.0%	4.7%	4.9%	4.0%	4.1%	4.2%

Figure 8.3 Gross and net profit

Figure 8.4 is a bar chart of the direct costs. Using a stacked bar like this makes it very easy to see the total of two sets of figures, and the proportion of one to the other.

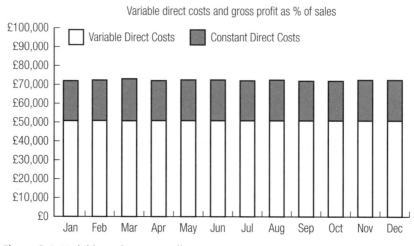

Figure 8.4 Variable and constant direct costs

Variable direct costs are about 71 per cent (50,000/70,000) of the total direct costs, and constant directs, therefore, are about 29 per cent.

On average constant direct costs are £21,000/month, and variable direct costs are £51,000/month, so a 10 per cent reduction of both would bring monthly reductions of £2,100 and £5,100 respectively. And, although for this exercise sales volumes are being held constant, it's worth bearing in mind that if sales volumes do increase, the savings from reduced constant direct costs will be unaffected, *while the savings on variable direct costs will also increase.*

We can show this by *temporarily* increasing sales volumes for Widgets Mk1 and Mk2 by 20 per cent, to 240/month and 120/month respectively, and looking again at the chart of direct costs.

Figure 8.5 shows that whilst the constant direct costs are of course unchanged, variable direct costs have increased and now represent about 75 per cent (60,000/80,000) of the total.

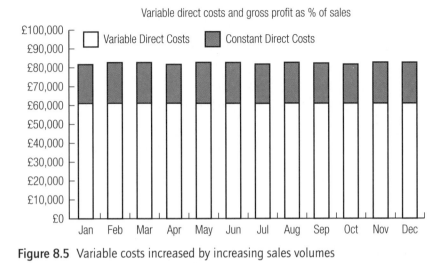

Figure 8.5 Variable costs increased by increasing sales volumes

Note: Change the sales volumes for Widgets Mk1 and Mk2 back to 200/month and 100/month respectively.

Therefore, the most productive costs to address initially are the variable directs, and of these, by far the greater portion of variable direct costs are for the widget parts. Their annual totals are £336,000 for the Mk1 and £192,000 for the Mk2.

OK – so by how much should the variable direct costs be reduced to increase gross profit from 24 per cent to 30 per cent by December? The formulae isn't simple, particularly as in practice the solution is likely to be a gradual change rather than a single one. It would be quicker now to use trial and error on the widget parts costs to achieve a gross profit of 30 per cent by December.

For those of you who are interested, here is a means of calculating what percentage reduction of variable direct costs is needed to increase gross profit from 24 per cent to 30 per cent as a single change.

For this formulae:

P = Percentage gross profit (%)

SR = Sales revenue (£140,000)

CD = Constant direct costs (£255,300)

VD = Variable direct costs (£610,800 initially)

$$P = \frac{SR - CD + VD}{SR} \times 100$$

$$\frac{P \times XR}{100} = SR - CD + VD$$

$$CD + VD = SR - \frac{P \times SR}{100}$$

$$VD = SR - \frac{P \times SR}{100} - CD$$

Substituting values for 30% gross profit:

$$VD = 1,140,000 - \frac{30 \times 1,140,000}{100} - 255,300$$

$$= 1,140,000 - 342,000 - 255,300$$

$$= 542,700$$

which is a variable direct costs reduction of 610,800 − 542,700 = **£68,100** or **11.15%**. The reduction of **total** variable costs necessary, including constants of £255,300, is (255,300 + 610,800) − (255,300 + 542,700) = **£68,100** or **7.9%**.

Trial and error

To work out what changes are needed to achieve a 30 per cent of sales gross profit by trial and error, and to introduce a smooth progression of reducing variable direct costs, simply replace the figure for widget parts costs with a reducing formulae from February onwards, check the result, and try again if necessary. To make it clearer, we'll go through the process once – see Figure 8.6.

	A	B	C
29	VARIABLE DIRECT COSTS / ITEM		
30	Parts for Widgets Mk1	140	=B30-(B30*.015)
31	Parts for Widgets Mk2	160	=B31-(B31*.015)
32	Diesel fuel (Deliveries)	8	8
33	Wages (Temporary staff)	15	15

Figure 8.6 Formulae for reducing widget parts costs

Let's suppose that we manage to find an alternative supplier of widget parts, who agrees to reduce the prices by 1.5 per cent, month on month, throughout the year. To examine the impact of this, enter the formulae **=B30–(B30*.015)** in C29 of the Budget Forecast, and copy it down to C30 and across to column M (Dec). Figure 8.6 shows the formulae in column C.

Figure 8.7 shows the effect of the price reduction on the cost of parts, and the total variable direct costs, throughout the year.

A	B	C	D	E	F	G	H	I	J	K	L	M	N
29 VARIABLE DIRECT COSTS / ITEM													
30 Parts for Widgets Mk1	140	138	136	134	132	130	128	126	124	122	120	119	
31 Parts for Widgets Mk2	160	158	155	153	151	148	146	144	142	140	138	135	
32 Diesel fuel (Deliveries)	8	8	8	8	8	8	8	8	8	8	8	8	
33 Wages (Temporary staff)	15	15	15	15	15	15	15	15	15	15	15	15	
34 (Spare)													
35													
36 VARIABLE DIRECT COSTS													
37 (Vol × Cost/Item)													
38 Parts for Widgets Mk1	28,000	27,580	27,166	26,759	26,357	25,962	25,573	25,189	24,811	24,439	24,072	23,711	309,620
39 Parts for Widgets Mk2	16,000	15,760	15,524	15,291	15,061	14,835	14,613	14,394	14,178	13,965	13,756	13,549	176,926
40 Diesel fuel (Deliveries)	2,400	2,400	2,400	2,400	2,400	2,400	2,400	2,400	2,400	2,400	2,400	2,400	28,800
41 Wages (Temporary staff)	4,500	4,500	4,500	4,500	4,500	4,500	4,500	4,500	4,500	4,500	4,500	4,500	54,000
42 (Spare)													
43 Total (C)	50,900	50,240	49,590	48,950	48,319	47,698	47,086	46,483	45,889	45,304	44,728	44,161	569,346

Figure 8.7 Reducing widget parts costs

The total variable direct costs have been reduced from £611,000 to £569,000, a reduction of £42,000 or 6.8 per cent.

The easiest way to view the gross profit is on a graph. Figure 8.8 shows the reducing variable direct costs together with the rising gross profit as a percentage of sales.

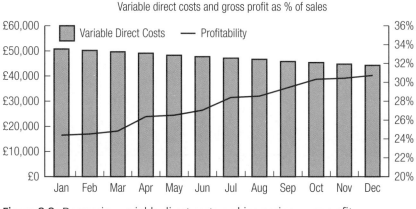

Figure 8.8 Decreasing variable direct costs and increasing gross profit

We can see that monthly gross profit is up to about 31 per cent by December; slightly exceeding the target we set ourselves of 30 per cent. The 'waves' in the gross profit line are the underlying effect of the constant direct costs for quarterly electricity and gas.

The next graph, in Figure 8.9, shows the same gross profit line – on a different scale – and also includes net profit, illustrating that the changes to gross profit also affect net profit.

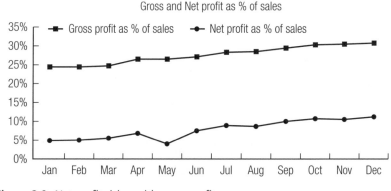

Figure 8.9 Net profit rising with gross profit

Whereas net profit through the year before the change was about 4 per cent of sales (this can be seen in Figure 8.3), it is now rising to around 11 per cent by December.

Finally, for this example, look at the effect these changes have had on cash flow by comparing Figure 8.10 with Figure 7.5.

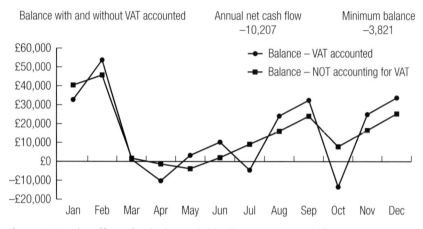

Figure 8.10 The effect of reducing variable direct cost on cash flow

Net cash flow is now more positive. The minimum balance, which was −£27,125 in October, is now only −£3,821 in May, and there is a healthy balance of about £25,000 at the year end, instead of an overdraft of about £25,000. Annual net cash flow has, of course, also improved by about £48,000.

If the overdraft represented a real bank account, and the interest due on borrowed money was being calculated in the cash flow model, then considerable savings from this would also be seen.

This example is finished – so set the parts costs for Widgets Mk1 and Mk2 in the budget forecast back to £140 and £160 respectively for the whole year.

Method 2

The change to a *cause* is known – what will be its effect?

Example 2 – The effect of increased overheads

In this example, an overhead cost rises half way through the year. We'll enter the change into the budget forecast and look at its effect.

⤴ brilliant reminder

Increased overheads reduce net profit and worsen cash flow.

Suppose that Salaries (Management) are due to rise from £17,000/month to £19,000/month from June onwards: what effect will this have? Of course, it will only take a few seconds to find out by simply changing the numbers, but let's first just work out what to expect. If it has no effect, then either basic understanding is at fault, or the model is wrong – both of which are worth knowing about!

From the 'cause and effect' summary (Figure 8.1), we know that increased overheads affect net profit and cash flow, but do not affect gross profit. Figure 8.3 shows that net profit, as a percentage of sales, averages about 4 per cent throughout the year with the original figures that were entered. So an increase in overheads from June onwards will reduce net profit over the same period.

Now, change Salaries (Management) to £19,000 from June onwards in the budget forecast. The effect on net profit can be seen in Figure 8.11. The dip in May is due to a one-off expense on building maintenance of £2,900, but the continuing level of around 2.5 per cent from June is the impact of the salaries increase. Note also that gross profit is unchanged at about 24 per cent.

Figure 8.11 The effect of increased overheads on net profit

Overhead changes also affect cash flow – see Figure 8.12. When compared to Figure 7.5, which is based on the original figures, net cash flow is now barely positive during the summer. Annual net cash flow has fallen to –£72,400, and the lowest balance has worsened to –£37,400 in December.

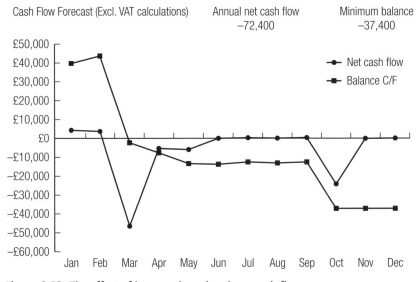

Figure 8.12 The effect of increased overheads on cash flow

This example is finished – set Salaries (Management) in the budget forecast back to £17,000 from June to December.

Further examples of cause and effect

Example 3 – Single large expenses: capital and start up

In Widget Makers Ltd, neither capital nor start up expenses are included in profit calculations, but they do of course have a most significant effect on cash flow.

Figure 8.13 shows the effect of removing the single payment capital expenses of:

- £50,000 for factory machinery in March
- £5,000 for office machinery in May
- £25,000 for office machinery in October.

This is a total of £80,000. So the annual net cash flow will be better by that amount compared with Figure 7.5, as will the closing bank balance at the year end.

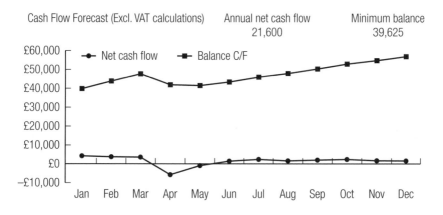

Figure 8.13 The effect on cash flow when removing capital expenditure

This example is finished – restore capital expenditure in the budget forecast to:

Factory machinery	Mar	50,000
Office machinery	May	5,000
" "	Oct	25,000

Example 4 – Increased constant direct costs

Constant direct costs affect gross profit, net profit and cash flow.

Suppose that Salaries (Widget production) increase to £22,000 from March onwards. Figure 8.14 shows that both gross and net profits fall to an average of around 22 per cent and 2.5 per cent respectively, although net *profit* has become a *loss* in May due to the building maintenance expense of £2,900.

Figure 8.14 The effect of increased constant direct costs on profit

The effect on cash flow is shown in Figure 8.15. Note that the picture is similar to that created by increased overheads; this is because both are fixed changes to regular monthly payments.

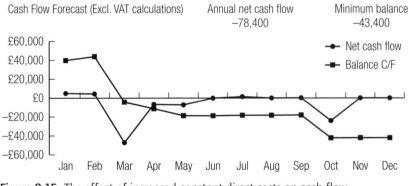

Figure 8.15 The effect of increased constant direct costs on cash flow

This example is finished – restore Salaries (Widget production) in the budget forecast to £20,000 from March onwards.

Example 5 – Simple timing changes

By simple timing changes, I mean those that are just a shift of an expense or revenue item, to another month. Timing changes during volume growth are more complex, and are dealt with in Chapter 10.

As the budget currently stands, there is a building maintenance expense of £2,900 in May. We'll examine what happens if, first of all, it is replanned for January, and secondly, for December.

1 January

The single building maintenance expense of £2,500 has been moved in the budget forecast from May back to January. Figure 8.16 shows that the gross profit line is unaffected (this is an overhead change), but that net profit is, as expected, reduced for January. It is important to note that *total net profit for the year is still the same*, because the total overhead expenditure has not altered.

Figure 8.16 The effect of an earlier single overhead expense on profit

Figure 8.17 shows the impact on cash flow. Because the payment has been brought forward to a time when cash reserves were plentiful, the effect compared with Figure 7.5 is almost undetectable, and both minimum balance and annual net cash flow are exactly the same.

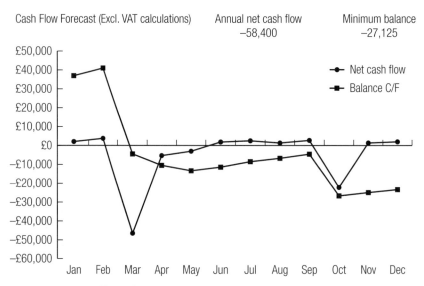

Figure 8.17 The effect of an earlier single overhead payment on cash flow

2 December

The single building maintenance expense of £2,900 has been moved forward to December. Again, save for a dip in net profit during that month, the overall net profit for the year is unchanged.

Cash flow, however, has not been affected a great deal, because the sum involved is not high compared with total expenditure, but it is noticeable. Figure 8.18 shows that although the annual net cash flow is unaltered (the same total amount of cash has flowed through the business during the year), the minimum balance during the year has improved to −£24,625 in December compared with −£27,125 in October (shown in Figure 7.5). This is because the minimum balance during October, seen in Figure 7.5, was partly due to the £2,900 building maintenance in May, which has now been moved beyond October to December.

This example is finished − restore building maintenance of £2,900 in the budget forecast to May, and all other months to £400.

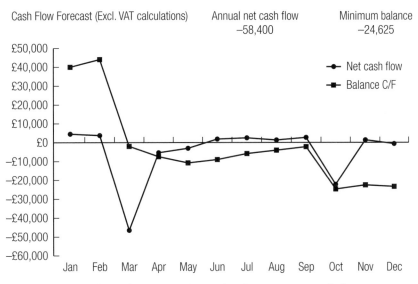

Figure 8.18 The effect of a later single overhead payment on cash flow

Example 6 – All change!

In this final example of simple cause and effect, every change – except for removal of capital expenditure – that has been made in the previous examples will be incorporated. These are:

- Reducing widget parts cost by 1.5 per cent from February. (Ex.1)
- Salaries (Management) increased to £19,000 from June. (Ex.2)
- Salaries (Widget production) increased to £22,000 from March. (Ex.4)
- One timing change – building maintenance of £2,900 moved from May to December.

Sales volume changes will be dealt with in Chapter 10.

Figure 8.19 and Figure 8.20 show the overall impact on profit and cash flow, respectively.

Figure 8.19 The effect of multiple changes on profit

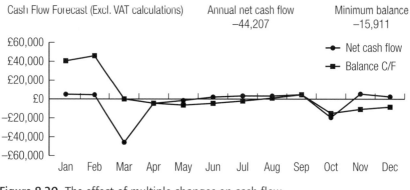

Figure 8.20 The effect of multiple changes on cash flow

This example is now finished – restore all of the changes for it:

1   Remove the reduction of widget parts cost by 1.5 per cent from February.

2   Restore Salaries (Management) to £17,000 for the year.

3   Restore Salaries (Widget production) to £20,000 for the year.

4   Move the building maintenance of £2,900 from December back to May and restore December to £400.

Gross profitability of each product

The sale price and parts cost of each of the widget types are not the same, and because parts cost affects gross profit, they are likely to generate different gross profit of sales percentages.

The new row headings and formulae for gross profit per product on the budget forecast are shown in Figure 8.21. These are already in the downloaded Completed Illustration Framework.

Note: If you are building it yourself only column B is illustrated; the column B formulae must be copied through to column M (Dec) with similar formula for the year totals.

	A	B
87	BY PRODUCT	
88	Widgets Mk1 – gross profit	=B13-B77
89	as % of sales	=B88/B13
90		
91	Widgets Mk2 – gross profit	=B14-B78
92	as % of sales	=B91/B14

Figure 8.21 Calculation of gross profit per product

A	B	C	D	E	F	G	H	I	J	K	L	M	N
86													
87 BY PRODUCT													
88 Widgets Mk1 – gross profit	13,100	12,850	12,650	13,100	12,850	12,750	13,100	12,850	13,000	13,100	12,850	12,750	154,950
89 as % of sales	23.8%	23.4%	23.0%	23.8%	23.4%	23.2%	23.8%	23.4%	23.6%	23.8%	23.4%	23.2%	23.5%
90													
91 Widgets Mk2 – gross profit	10,100	9,850	9,650	10,100	9,850	9,750	10,100	9,850	10,000	10,100	9,850	9,750	118,950
92 as % of sales	25.3%	24.6%	24.1%	25.3%	24.6%	24.4%	25.3%	24.6%	25.0%	25.3%	24.6%	24.4%	24.8%

Figure 8.22 Gross profit per product

The gross profits per product from the new formulae are shown in Figure 8.22. Focus on the percentage of sales figures.

Both Widgets Mk1 and Mk2 are producing a gross profit of about 24 per cent on sales. Let's try reducing the variable costs for one of them – Widgets Mk2 – and see what the impact is.

In the budget forecast put **=B31-(B31*0.015)** in C31, and copy it across to column M.

Figure 8.23 shows the gross profit percentage of sales for both widget types.

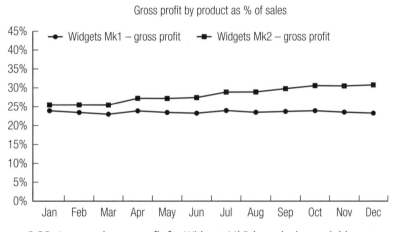

Figure 8.23 Increased gross profit for Widgets Mk2 by reducing variable costs

Note that the Mk2 profit has risen by about 6 per cent.

This *example is now finished* – restore the parts cost of Widgets Mk2 to its original value of £160.

Summary

In this chapter we have:

- understood the purpose of the reiterative process;
- explored the practical aspects of how to examine the effect of changes;
- seen a number of simple cause and effects that will be met in budget and cash flow forecasts;
- added new rows to the budget forecast for calculating gross and net profit;
- tried several examples of simple cause and effect on the illustration computer models, including one that combined most of them in one forecast;
- created additional formulae on the budget forecast for calculating the individual gross profit of each widget type.

CHAPTER 9

Allocation, monitoring and reviewing

This chapter is about ...

The importance, for the purpose of monitoring and reviewing forecasts, of considering the visibility, clarity and relevance of forecasts for different types of users, and what can happen if they are not given sufficient attention.

We'll look at budget allocation and performance monitoring principles, and put in place monitoring for Widget Makers Ltd.

Visibility, clarity and relevance

A forecast conceived and built by the best possible people, based upon the best possible strategy, using the best possible forecasting, costing and budgetary techniques is of no use whatever if it doesn't provide clear and relevant information to those who need it.

Visibility of forecasting and cost control systems, with the information they provide, should underpin the decisions of not just top management and the financial departments, but equally importantly those of all managers in their day-to-day running of the business.

Critical to the success of financial forecasting and cost control systems are ensuring that they provide:

- the right information
- to the right people
- at the right time.

Visibility

A key objective is to inform the business decisions of those concerned with day-to-day operations right through to those responsible for strategic business development. But if the plans and forecasts are not visible to those who make the decisions, then this key objective has not been met.

Perhaps this sounds all too obvious? Maybe, but whilst it is clear and obvious that those involved in strategic decisions must be aware of the strategic business plans, what are often overlooked are the reasons for keeping those not obviously involved in strategic plans informed of them. Apart from general motivation it is surprising how many apparently isolated day-to-day decisions are influenced by knowing what's coming up in the next few months, or even next year. This also extends to departmental budget forecasts and allocations.

The more people that are made aware of plans and forecasts, the more likely they are to respond to them. In any event, the converse is certainly true – if nothing is known of plans or budgets then managers can hardly be held accountable for any incompatible decisions they make.

Clarity

Edward de Bono, in his book *The Mechanism of Mind* (published by Jonathan Cape, 1969) says:

'Matters are often made more and more complex by the ability of man to play elaborate games that feed on themselves to create bewildering structures of immense intricacy, which obscure rather than reveal.'

We've all seen it far too often. And ironically it is the inappropriate application of the very technology that should make things easier for us that is largely to blame for much of the over complication that is thrust upon us.

With a spreadsheet, for example, it's all too easy to create complex interlinked structures and break them down into self-contained modules for data entry, which are then to be re-assembled as an integrated whole. Much like taking a picture and cutting it up to make a jigsaw. Creating the spreadsheet or making the jigsaw is a relatively easy operation, but putting either of them back together again is quite another matter!

Another problem is that of obscure and remote relationships between the output from a system and the realities it is supposed to represent. It's all very well to develop what might be an extremely elegant and indeed accurate mathematical model of the dynamic behaviour of a complex business, but if the output from the system cannot be readily related to the decision makers then it should stay in the halls of academia.

Having said that, ongoing development of business management techniques will often require complex and academic research, and it's in the interests of the commercial world to encourage such work – but be careful not to get befuddled by it or removed from reality.

brilliant tip

Managers should keep things as simple as possible consistent with providing sufficient and clear information for the level of visibility and control needed, academics should do all that they can to make their work as accessible as they can to the routine matter of running a business.

Relevance

Perhaps having just implied 'the more information the better', a little balance and focus would be appropriate. Relevance in the context of plans, forecasts and budgets is about what is useful and meaningful, ideally providing *everything that is needed* and *nothing that is not*.

Managers of different disciplines and at different levels in the business require information specific to their responsibilities and in appropriate detail so that they can readily absorb what they need and where necessary act on it.

As a general principle for routine information:

● the higher the level of the recipient the broader and shallower the information to be provided;
● the lower the level the narrower and deeper the routine information.

As shown in Figure 9.1.

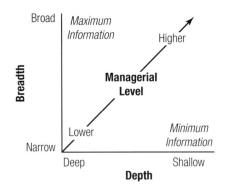

Figure 9.1 Balancing breadth and depth of routine information

Ideally, the information systems should be able to provide all routine reports from the same set of basic data.

For most non-routine information – where for example board members require more detailed information about a particular product – if the information systems are well structured the board should require nothing more than one of the 'narrower and deeper' reports already in existence at the appropriate level.

We should be able to create other non-routine reports, at any level, required by any managers or their staff.

Getting away with it? No!

It is an unfortunate fact that certain aspects of a business can appear to be functioning well, especially in the short term, whilst flying in the face of plans and forecasts which have not been communicated to the appropriate people: the 'invisibility' factor.

Exactly the same is true of actual expenditure and revenue details which are either not communicated at all, or communicated too late to enable timely corrective action to be taken.

Occasional lapses of communication are likely to be absorbed without significant impact by both the business and those whose work is directly affected. On the other hand, frequent occurrences will have a serious impact both on the business and people, aggravated by the probability, and certainly the perception, that such 'lapses' are due to deficiencies in the company culture and practice at a senior level – or perhaps because the plans and forecasts don't exist at all – in either case the effect will be the same.

In the short term an individual, a department or an entire small business can appear to function satisfactorily in an environment of inadequate communication of plans, forecasts and budget information. But in the longer term some or all of the following *will* arise:

- low or insupportable profitability;
- cash flow difficulties;
- poor service;
- low quality products;
- de-motivation of managers and staff;
- reduced faith in, and loyalty to, the management team.

Conversely, where a business is already experiencing these sorts of problems, the communication of plans, forecasts and budgetary information is essential as part of the rehabilitation process.

Budget allocation

So, bearing the above in mind the forecast has been built, checked, rechecked, revised and finally declared to be the best view of the year ahead that can be obtained. It has, therefore, achieved the status of an operational budget and is ready for allocation.

Operational budget status usually means that:

- fixed (capital, start up, constant direct and overhead) costs for each period must not be exceeded;
- intrinsic sales volumes for each period must be achieved;
- variable direct costs must not exceed the value determined by their arithmetic relationship with achieved sales volumes;
- a change can only be authorised by the budget's controller.

Of course, every company can, and will, determine precisely what a budget allocation means in its own organisation. As always in these matters, there is no right or wrong.

We can split the budget into departmental responsibilities, or maintain it as a single entity. If split, we still have the option of either actually dividing the allocation up into departmental extracts, or keeping it as a single entity that every department receives, but in which their specific responsibilities are clearly identified.

The deciding factors when choosing are usually:

● the physical size and geographical split of the business;
● the size and complexity of individual departmental responsibilities;
● company policy.

Performance monitoring principles

I make no apology for once again repeating the only certainty of budget forecasts – they are wrong. Consequently, they must be checked, reviewed and amended to ensure that they represent reality – or, rather, that they are as close to reality as possible.

Frequency of monitoring

In theory the frequency of checks and reviews depends to a large extent on the nature of the business, its financial dynamics and the inherent probability of significant variations occurring in a given period. All very technical! In practice it's usually very easy to decide the minimum interval between checks. In fact, this has probably been decided for you, unless you are responsible for book-keeping policy, because that is where the actual data against which the forecast is compared will probably come from.

When all is said and done, just about any business will benefit from, and not be overburdened by, a calendar-monthly monitoring cycle.

Widget Makers Ltd chose a calendar-monthly period.

The source of actual figures

> ### brilliant tip
>
> The principle of monitoring is simply to compare what has actually been spent or earned with what was forecast. This is why it is so important when you create the budget that you align expense and revenue headings with the source of actual figures, and that their periodicity is the same.

If elements are broken down in different ways, or do not use the same periods, comparison is at best very difficult, or at worst impossible.

The source of the actual performance figures depends on the way in which each company operates, but you usually get them from either the ledgers of the company's accounts – explained in Chapter 5 – or something similar that has been established for the purpose.

Widget Makers Ltd use the ledgers as the source of their actual figures.

> Note: From here, references to the ledgers should be taken to include any other system that provides similar facilities, specifically details of purchase and sales *invoices*, and purchase and sales *payments*.

Invoices or payments?

In Chapter 1, the offset in time between when an expense is incurred, and cash is paid out for it, was explained, as was the similar offset between a sale and receipt of payment. And, of course, that these timing differences exist is the main reason for having a cash flow forecast at all.

So, when collecting actual figures, should they be 'expense incurred' and 'sale made' – the *invoice* stage – or 'expense paid' and 'income received' – the *payment* stage – or both, or some combination of both?

Dealing with the straightforward circumstances first:

(a) If there is no cash flow forecast, then clearly there is little purpose in collecting cash payment and receipt figures. Actual data must be *invoice* details.

(b) Even if there is a cash flow forecast, but actual cash flow information is not available, then again there is no choice – actual data has to be *invoice* details.

(c) If invoice details are not available, then only *payment* details can be used.

Circumstance (a) presents no problem at all and will be fairly common in departments of larger companies.

Circumstance (b) is also fully workable, providing it is acceptable that the cash flow forecast can only ever be regarded as an indication of likely reality, but not as an accurate representation. Again, you'll find this situation in departments of larger companies, especially those that like their managers to be aware of the cash flow implications of the department's work.

Circumstance (c) will only be of practical forecasting use in a business that deals *exclusively* in cash or only *always* pays invoices immediately they are received, and obtains immediate payment for its products. I can't think of any business that would meet these criteria and therefore we'll ignore (c).

And then there is a more complicated scenario:

(d) With full access to the ledgers both *invoice* and *payment* details are available, and either or both may be used for monitoring purposes.

Circumstance (d) is the most likely to be found in medium to small companies, of which Widget Makers Ltd is an example.

The way in which the actual figures, whether *invoice* or *payment*, are recorded is dealt with later in this chapter.

Comparing actual figures with the allocated budget

This section describes three fundamental ways in which we can compare actual figures with the allocated budget. The objective of them all is to retain a copy of the allocation, and to update the original copy with actual figures. The three methods are:

1   Paper budget copy.

2   Forecast spreadsheet copies.

3   Key figure copies.

Before looking at these, I'll mention another format that may be familiar to you, and which you may want to try, especially if you have 'paper forecast' experience. It's also a format sometimes used in advice packs to new business starters, *but it is not recommended for spreadsheet-based forecasts.* Figure 9.2 illustrates the principle.

	A	B	C	D	E	F	G
1	FILE : FIG9						
2	28/10/1997						
3			Jan		Feb		Mar
4		F'cst	Act	F'cst	Act	F'cst	Act
5							
6	Cost item 1	158	165	237	198	132	
7	Cost item 2	53	48	80	73	44	
8	Cost item 3	92	92	138	126	77	
9	Cost item 4	354	344	531	564	295	
10	Cost item 5	16	20	24	27	13	
11							
12	Totals	673	669	1010	988	561	0

Figure 9.2 A format *not* recommended for spreadsheet forecasts

The idea is to place the actual figures alongside their forecast values by dividing each month's column into two. On a spreadsheet we must use two separate columns but there are problems with using this format on a spreadsheet.

Take the year totals for example. Consider row 8 of Figure 9.2 for which the formulae for the *forecast* year total would be:

=B8 + D8 + F8 + H8 + J8 + L8 + N8 + P8 + R8 + T8 + V8 + X8

The SUM function can't be used because every alternate column must be skipped. Similarly, the *actual* year total for the same row would be:

=C8 + E8 + G8 + I8 + K8 + M8 + O8 + Q8 + S8 + U8 + W8 + Y8

And any other function that depends on a contiguous sequence of cells couldn't be used either – *average* for instance.

Hopefully, I've persuaded you not to use this format. Now here are three viable methods.

1. Paper budget copy

A very easy way to keep a copy of the allocation – print a copy of each of the models on paper. That's it – job done!

2. Spreadsheet forecast copies

This method looks complicated in its description, but in fact it can be done in just two or three minutes, certainly faster than I'll be able to write down how to do it.

The aim is to have three copies of each forecast on the same spreadsheet, one above the other. So each model's spreadsheet (Sales, Budget and Cash Flow) will look like it does in Figure 9.3.

Operational	For update with actuals
(As built)	
Fixed	
Original figures	Original figures for
(No formulae)	comparison
Variance	
Headings and variance	Difference (variance)
formulae	between operational
	and original figures

Figure 9.3 Three copies of the forecasts

Here is a way of creating the two additional copies, *but don't do it now*, read through for understanding, and return to it later if you need to.

1   Make a copy of the model below the 'operational', but *omit the formulae; copy the values only*. It is best to leave a reasonable number of rows empty between the bottom of the 'operational' and the top of the 'fixed' copy; perhaps 10 or so, to lessen the risk of confusion between them.

2 Now, below the 'fixed' copy, again leaving some spare rows, make a copy of the row and column titles.

- The *top version* is the operational one, and will be updated with actual figures where they are not picked up by the linking.

- The *middle version* contains the fixed original figures; they will not be changed.

- The *bottom version* – which at the moment consists of only the row and column headings – will be used to compare the actual figures in the 'operational' with the original figures in the 'fixed' version.

To do this, note the cell addresses of the first data row for January in the operational and fixed versions. Then in the corresponding cell of the variance version, enter a formulae that subtracts one from the other. Finally copy the formulae down the rows and across the columns of the variance version. Figure 9.4 illustrates the principle.

	A	B	. . . etc	
6	65			Operational – for
7	153			update with actuals
8	46			
	A	B	. . . etc	
106	72			Fixed – original figures
107	153			for comparison
108	37			
	A	B	. . . etc	
206	7	[=A6–A106]		Variances – calculates
207	0	[=A7–A107]		difference between fixed
208	0	[=A8–A108]		and operational figures

Figure 9.4 Formulae to calculate variance

Initially the variance version will display all zeros, because the operational and fixed versions are still identical. As soon as anything is changed in the operational version, however, the difference between them and the fixed original figures will be displayed.

3. Key figure copy

This method uses exactly the same principle as 'budget copy', except that instead of keeping a copy of all of the original figures, only those of major significance are kept for comparison with actuals. For instance, the total sales volume and value, each of the cost category subtotals, and the total cost.

So the steps for this method are very similar to 'budget copy', except that only the key figure rows are reproduced for the fixed and variance versions.

The pros and cons of each method

1. Paper copy

This has the advantage of being extremely easy to set up, but the disadvantage that manual methods must be used to calculate variances when actual figures are recorded on the spreadsheet.

2. Forecast spreadsheet copies

This has the advantage of spreadsheet-calculated variances in full detail, but the disadvantage of being a little cumbersome and perhaps over-detailed, especially if the spreadsheets are large.

3. Key figure copy

This has the advantage of spreadsheet-calculated variances, and is much less cumbersome than the full budget copy. Its only real disadvantage is that you can't get fully detailed variances from it.

Choosing a method

I suggest you use a combination of 'paper copy' and 'key figure copy'. This will provide automatic calculation of key variances, and if more detail is required, manual comparisons can be made between actual figures and the paper copy for any individual heading.

Setting up monitoring for the Widget Makers Ltd forecast

Widget Makers Ltd has chosen to use the combination of 'paper copy' and 'key figure copy' and so the first job is to make a paper copy of the allocated sales, budget and cash flow and put it to one side for use later.

Once that is done, the spreadsheet models can be set up. Again, the detail of a written description can look a little daunting, but it really doesn't take more than about 15 minutes, with perhaps another 15 to 'tidy things up and make it look good', and to test that everything works properly.

> **Note:** The monitoring copies of everything described here are already on Completed Illustration Framework.xls.

Sales forecast

1 Copy row 11 'Total Volume' to row 31. Only the values (figures) are wanted, not the formulae.

2 Copy row 21 'Total Value' to row 33 – again, just the values.

3 Put the label 'ORIGINAL FIXED' in A28.

And that is the fixed original copy of the operational sales volumes and values. Because there are no formulae, they will not change, whatever happens elsewhere. Now for the variances block.

1 Copy rows 28 to 33 to row 37.

2 Replace the label in A37 with 'VARIANCES (Actual – Fixed Original)'.

3 Using the formulae below, subtract the figures in the middle (fixed) block from their corresponding figures in the top (operational) block:

In B40 enter **=B11–B31**

In B42 enter **=B21–B33**

and copy them both across to column N (Year Totals).

And that's it. Now, if any of the total volume or total value figures in the operational block are not the same as their corresponding figures in the fixed original block, their difference will be shown in the variance block. Figure 9.5 shows the two new blocks for the sales forecast.

A	B	C	D	E	F	G	H	I	J	K	L	M	N
28 **ORIGINAL FIXED**													
29 *** SALES ***	Jan	Feb	Mar	Apr	May	Jun	Jul	Aug	Sep	Oct	Nov	Dec	Year Total
30													
31 Total Volume	300	300	300	300	300	300	300	300	300	300	300	300	3600
32													
33 Total Value £	95,000	95,000	95,000	95,000	95,000	95,000	95,000	95,000	95,000	95,000	95,000	95,000	1,140,000
34													
35													
36													
37 **VARIANCES (Actual – Fixed Original)**													
38 *** SALES ***	Jan	Feb	Mar	Apr	May	Jun	Jul	Aug	Sep	Oct	Nov	Dec	Year Total
39													
40 Total Volume	0	0	0	0	0	0	0	0	0	0	0	0	0
41													
42 Total Value £	0	0	0	0	0	0	0	0	0	0	0	0	0

Figure 9.5 Performance monitoring blocks – sales

Budget forecast

To make a copy of the key figure rows in the budget, either copy each row individually – in the same way as for the sales forecast – or, and this is the easiest way, copy all of the rows in one go and then delete those in the fixed original copy that are not wanted to leave the rows shown in Figure 9.6.

	A	
111	ORIGINAL FIXED	
112		
113		
114	SALES	
115		Total volume
116		
117		Total £ Value
118		
119	CAPITAL COSTS	
120		Total (A)
121		
122	START UP COSTS	
123		Total (B)
124		
125	VARIABLE DIRECT COSTS	
126		Total (C)
127		
128	CONSTANT DIRECT COSTS	
129		Total (D)
130		
131	OVERHEADS	
132		Total (E)
133		
134	TOTAL COSTS	
135	(A + B + C + D + E)	
136		Total (F)

Figure 9.6 Key figure headings for the budget forecast

That completes the copy of the fixed original key figures of the budget forecast.

The variance block is going to have exactly the same key figure headings as the fixed block, and so that's the best place to copy it from so as – to replicate the column A labels shown in Figure 9.6 with the label 'VARI-ANCES (Actual – Fixed Original)' at the top of the block.

As in the sales forecast, enter formulae throughout the variance block, including the year totals, to subtract fixed block figures from their corresponding positions in the operational block. The formulae for Completed Illustration Framework.xls are shown in Figure 9.7.

	A	B	C	D	E	F
143	VARIANCES (Actual – Fixed Original)					
144						
145						
146	SALES					
147	Total volume	B11-B115	C11-C115	D11-D115	E11-E115	F11-F115
148						
149	Total £ Value	B16-B117	C16-C117	D16-D117	E16-E117	F16-F117
150						
151	CAPITAL COSTS					
152	Total (A)	B22-B120	C22-C120	D22-D120	E22-E120	F22-F120
153						
154	START UP COSTS					
155	Total (B)	B27-B123	C27-C123	D27-D123	E27-E123	F27-F123
156						
157	VARIABLE DIRECT COSTS					
158	Total (C)	B43-B126	C43-C126	D43-D126	E43-E126	F43-F126
159						
160	CONSTANT DIRECT COSTS					
161	Total (D)	B52-B129	C52-C129	D52-D129	E52-E129	F52-F129
162						
163	OVERHEADS					
164	Total (E)	B65-B132	C65-C132	D65-D132	E65-E132	F65-F132
165						
166	TOTAL COSTS					
167	(A + B + C + D + E)					
168	Total (F)	B69-B136	C69-C136	D69-D136	E69-E136	F69-F136

Figure 9.7 Variance formulae for the budget forecast

In the budget forecast another variance block is needed if there are variable direct costs, one that will compare the actual variable direct costs with the forecast value/item factor. For example, in our forecast, the 'Diesel fuel for deliveries' factor is £8 per widget sold. But sales volumes will never be exactly as forecast, and it's highly improbable that the cost of diesel fuel per widget will precisely match the forecast factor.

Our aim, therefore, is to monitor any variable direct cost factors to check that they are about right. Several months' figures may be necessary to establish the trend. If any significant variance is noted, then of course we can adjust the factors for the remaining months of the forecast.

The additional block is 'Variable direct variances' and can be put below the 'Variances' block. It needs to have the headings of each of the variable direct costs.

Steps

The formulae are needed to subtract the forecast cost per item from the actual cost per item. Remember that 'Diesel fuel' and 'Wages (Temporary staff)' operate on the total widget volumes.

Create the labels and formulae as shown in Figure 9.8: the row numbers are the same as in the layout of Completed Illustration Framework.xls.

	A	B	C
174	VARIABLE DIRECT VARIANCES		
175		Jan	Feb
176			
177	VARIABLE DIRECT COSTS / ITEM		
178	Parts for Widgets Mk1	=(B38/B8)-B30	=(C38/C8)-C30
179	Parts for Widgets Mk2	=(B39/B9)-B31	=(C39/C9)-C31
180	Diesel fuel (Deliveries)	=(B40/B11)-B32	=(C40/C11)-C32
181	Wages (Temporary staff)	=(B41/B11)-B33	=(C41/C11)-C33

Figure 9.8 Row headings and formulae for variable direct variances

Because the numbers displayed may be less than 1, format the block to two decimal places.

Now, if any of the actual factors are different to the forecast values, and in practice they almost certainly will be, the difference will be displayed in this block.

Cash flow forecast

All of the necessary key figure information for the cash flow forecast is contained within its 'Cash Flow and Bank' section.

1 Copy rows 59 to 66 to row 96 (values only, the formulae are not wanted).

2 Add the label 'ORIGINAL FIXED' in A94.

That completes the copy of the fixed original block for the cash flow forecast. The variance block is going to have exactly the same key figure headings as the fixed block.

1 Copy rows 96 to 103 to row 109.

2 Enter the label 'VARIANCES (Actual – Fixed Original)' in A107.

3 As before, enter formulae throughout the variances block, including the year totals, to subtract fixed block figures from their corresponding positions in the operational block. The formulae are shown in Figure 9.9.

And that completes the monitoring blocks for the cash flow forecast.

The spreadsheets are now ready to receive actual performance figures.

	A	B	C	D	E	F	G
94	ORIGINAL FIXED						
95							
96	CASH FLOW AND BANK						
97							
98	Net cash flow	4,625	4,000	−46,075	−5,375	−5,700	1,925
99							
100	Balance B/F	35,000	39,625	43,625	−24,50	−7,825	−13,525
101	Cash In	95,000	95,000	95,000	95,000	95,000	95,000
102	Cash Out	90,375	91,000	141,075	100,375	100,700	93,075
103	Balance C/F	39,625	43,625	−2,450	−7,825	−13,525	−11,600
104							
105							
106							
107	VARIANCES (Actual – Fixed Original)						
108							
109	CASH FLOW AND BANK						
110							
111	Net cash flow	=B61-B98	=C61-C98	=D61-D98	=E61-E98	=F61-F98	=G61-G98
112							
113	Balance B/F	=B63-B100	=C63-C100	=D63-D100	=E63-E100	=F63-F100	=G63-G100
114	Cash In	=B64-B101	=C64-C101	=D64-D101	=E64-E101	=F64-F101	=G64-G101
115	Cash Out	=B65-B102	=C65-C102	=D65-D102	=E65-E102	=F65-F102	=G65-G102
116	Balance C/F	=B66-B103	=C66-C103	=D66-D103	=E66-E103	=F66-F103	=G66-G103

Figure 9.9 The monitoring blocks and formulae for the cash flow

Recording actual figures

Earlier on, we considered the question of whether to record actual *invoices* or *payments* and found this partly depended on which were available. For Widget Makers Ltd we'll assume that both are available from the ledgers, but the methods described here will be equally applicable to any circumstance.

Table 9.1 Widget Makers Ltd – January period end actual figures

SALES	
Widget Mk1 sales volumes	206
Widget Mk2 sales volumes	92
Widget Mk1 sales value	56,650
Widget Mk2 sales value	36,800
EXPENSES	
Capital costs	
Factory machinery	–
Office machinery	–
Start up costs	
Design of Widget Mk3	–
Variable direct costs	
Parts for Widgets Mk1	28,840
Parts for Widgets Mk2	14,720
Diesel fuel (Deliveries)	2,450
Wages (Temporary staff)	3,900
Constant direct costs	
Electricity	–
Gas	–
Machine maintenance (Factory)	600
Salaries (Widget production)	19,750
Vehicle maintenance (Delivery)	3,500
Overheads	
Building maintenance	150
Machine maintenance (Office)	100
Petrol (Managers' cars)	550
Postage	25
Rates	200
Salaries (Management)	17,000
Stationery	210
Telephone	–
Vehicle maintenance (Managers)	

Rather than looking at the theory, it is probably best to run through the collection and recording of one month's actual figures from beginning to end. We may as well start with January.

Early in February the following actual performance figures for January become available. All revenue and expense items are *invoice* figures, not cash payments or receipts. And don't forget, the figures do *not* include VAT.

To update the forecast then, it is just a matter of entering these figures in place of the forecast values for January.

Note: In the downloaded file pack the spreadsheet 'Actual figures entered in the Completed Illustration Framework.xls' already has the actual figures for January entered.

brilliant tip

Sometimes forecast figures occur in more than one place, for instance 'Sales Volume' and 'Sales Value' are in the sales forecast *and* in the budget forecast. The rule is to overwrite the forecast at the lowest point in the system's hierarchy, and allow the links to update any dependants. In the case of the sales figures, this is the sales forecast tab. The links will automatically update the budget forecast.

Steps

1 Enter the actual sales volume and value figures in Sales Forecast. Note that the actual sales values are identical to the forecast once the actual volumes are in. This is because the widgets were sold at the expected price. However, it's a good discipline to nevertheless overwrite the formulae that is calculating the value with the actual figure, because it can then be clearly seen at a later date that the actual figures for the month *were* considered.

2   Enter the actual expenses in Budget Forecast. Again, where the actual is the same as a calculated forecast figure, overwrite the formulae with the actual figure. And where there is no actual figure where one was forecast, enter a zero.

And that's it, all of the month's actual figures in, and it only took about five minutes. The next job is to *look* at the forecast and see what it tells us.

Reviewing the forecast

The word *look* in the last sentence is highlighted for a very good reason: it is stressing the importance of studying the results of actual data entry, of looking for the tell-tale signs that things are progressing satisfactorily, or going wrong. It's unlikely that this will be a problem when you first start to use the forecast – it's new, and you will probably spend hours exploring the first month or two of results.

brilliant disaster

But here is the danger. It usually takes a few months of actual data entry before steady trends are established, or before the factors and assumptions start to reveal their inherent errors. Before that point is reached, and the novelty of having all this financial control information available starts to wear off, the monthly review may have become so routine that you only give the results a cursory glance before consigning them to a file.

Worse – much, much worse. You may even have delegated monthly data entry to someone who has no responsibility for, or expertise in, what the forecasts are showing. Disaster!

If you really, absolutely, categorically, positively, 'no other way' must delegate the monthly data entry (it only takes a few minutes, for goodness sake) to someone else, then it's even more important that you look, really look, each month, at the forecasts as soon as the latest figures have been entered. Or you could find yourself in real trouble.

There are no special rules for what to look at – every company and every forecast is different. But you *will* see when things are going wrong, so long as you look carefully. And there is no better way of keeping in tune with the figures, line by line, than by entering the monthly figures yourself. Don't regard it as simply one of those 'easy' jobs that can be given to the office junior – these are the life blood details of the company, and they deserve your personal attention and expertise in their analysis.

OK – enough of the preaching, let's get back to *looking* at what has happened to the Widget Makers Ltd forecast now that the first month's figures are in – see Figure 9.10.

6		Jan	Feb	Mar	Apr	May
7	SALES					
8	Volume – Widgets Mk1	**206**	200	200	200	200
9	Volume – Widgets Mk2	**92**	100	100	100	100
10	(Spare)					
11	Total volume	**298**	300	300	300	300
12						
13	Value – Widgets Mk1	**56,650**	55,000	55,000	55,000	55,000
14	Value – Widgets Mk2	**36,800**	40,000	40,000	40,000	40,000
15	(Spare)					
16	Total £ Value	**93,450**	95,000	95,000	95,000	95,000
17						
18	CAPITAL COSTS					
19	Factory machinery			50,000		
20	Office machinery					5,000
21	(Spare)					
22	Total (A)	0	0	50,000	0	5,000
23						
24	START UP COSTS					
25	Design of Widget Mk3				10,000	2,000
26	(Spare)					
27	Total (B)	0	0	0	10,000	2,000
28						
29	VARIABLE DIRECT COSTS / ITEM					
30	Parts for Widgets Mk1	140	140	140	140	140
31	Parts for Widgets Mk2	160	160	160	160	160
32	Diesel fuel (Deliveries)	8	8	8	8	8
33	Wages (Temporary staff)	15	15	15	15	15
34	(Spare)					
35						

Figure 9.10 The budget with actual figures entered

	Jan	Feb	Mar	Apr	May
36 VARIABLE DIRECT COSTS					
37 (Vol × Cost / Item)					
38 Parts for Widgets Mk1	**28,840**	28,000	28,000	28,000	28,000
39 Parts for Widgets Mk2	**14,720**	16,000	16,000	16,000	16,000
40 Diesel fuel (Deliveries)	**2,450**	2,400	2,400	2,400	2,400
41 Wages (Temporary staff)	**3,900**	4,500	4,500	4,500	4,500
42 (Spare)					
43 Total (C)	**49,910**	50,900	50,900	50,900	50,900
44					
45 CONSTANT DIRECT COSTS					
46 Electricity				500	500
47 Gas			900		
48 Machine maintenance (Factory)	600	600	600	600	600
49 Salaries (Widget production)	**19,750**	20,000	20,000	20,000	20,000
50 Vehicle maintenance (Delivery)	**3,500**	300	300	300	300
51 (Spare)					
52 Total (D)	**23,850**	21,400	21,800	20,900	21,400
53					
54 OVERHEADS					
55 Building maintenance	**150**	400	400	400	2,900
56 Machine maintenance (Office)	**100**	100	100	100	100
57 Petrol (Manager's cars)	**550**	600	600	600	600
58 Postage	**25**	90	90	90	90
59 Rates	200			**200**	**200**
60 Salaries (Management)	17,000	17,000	17,000	17,000	17,000
61 Stationery	**210**	85	85	85	85
62 Telephone		325			325
63 Vehicle maintenance (Managers)	0	100	100	100	100
64 (Spare)					
65 Total (E)	**18,235**	18,700	18,375	18,575	21,400
66					
67 TOTAL COSTS					
68 (A + B + C + D + E)					
69 Total (F)	**91,995**	91,000	141,075	100,375	100,700

Figure 9.10 Continued

All of the relevant information is in the budget forecast. The figures that are different to the original (Figure 7.2) are in bold characters.

Now, the fact that many of the figures are different is no surprise at all – the majority will vary from the forecast every month. What's important is by *how much* they are different, and of course that is why we've included the calculation of variance blocks. Not only do they show that a variance exists, but also the magnitude of it.

Budget variances

Figure 9.11 shows the budget forecast's variance and variable direct variance blocks. My spreadsheet is set up to show negative values in brackets, they stand out that way more than a minus sign.

Note that in all cases a *negative variance* means that the actual is *less* than the original budget.

Let's now look at each of the key figure variances.

Total sales volume

Under budget by 2 in 300, but no cause for concern here. Though we do note from the detail in Figure 9.10 that Widgets Mk2 volumes were 8 under budget – that's a 4 per cent forecast error. Look at this carefully next month.

Total sales value

Under budget by £1,550 – exactly as expected for the sales volumes achieved.

Capital

No expenditure as forecast.

Start up

No expenditure as forecast.

143	VARIANCES (Actual − Fixed Original)		
144			
145			
146	SALES		
147	Total volume	(	2)
148			
149	Total £ Value	(	1550)
150			
151	CAPITAL COSTS		
152	Total (A)		
153			
154	START UP COSTS		
155	Total (B)		
156			
157	VARIABLE DIRECT COSTS		
158	Total (C)	(	990)
159			
160	CONSTANT DIRECT COSTS		
161	Total (D)	2950	
162			
163	OVERHEADS		
164	Total (E)	(	340)
165			
166	TOTAL COSTS		
167	(A + B + C + D + E)		
168	Total (F)	1620	
169			
170			
171			
172			
173			
174	VARIABLE DIRECT VARIANCES		
175			
176			
177	VARIABLE DIRECT COSTS / ITEM		
178	Parts for Widgets Mk1		
179	Parts for Widgets Mk2		
180	Diesel fuel (Deliveries)	.22	
181	Wages (Temporary staff)	(1.91)	

Figure 9.11 The budget's variance blocks reflecting January actual data

Variable direct costs

Under budget by £990. A lower figure would be expected in view of the below forecast volumes, but is all of it due to volume? It could be worked out, but there is no need – the variable direct variances will tell us when we look at them.

Constant direct costs

Over budget by £2,950 – that's quite a lot, and we can't see from the key figure variances what has caused it. But by looking back to the original budget (Figure 7.2) and comparing the figures for constant directs in January, we see that whilst Salaries (Widget production) are under budget by £250, Vehicle maintenance (Delivery) is over budget by £3,200. Speaking to the transport manager reveals that one of the vans needed a new engine.

Overheads

Under budget by £340, not really a big enough variance to get concerned about, though out of interest a quick glance down the paper original (Figure 7.2) shows that the variances were:

Building maintenance	(250)
Petrol (Managers' cars)	(50)
Postage	(65)
Stationery	125
Vehicle maintenance (Mgrs)	(100)

Total costs

The net effect of all of the cost variances is £1,620 over budget.

Now to look at those variable direct variances.

Parts for Widgets Mk1 and Mk2

No variance – the parts costs were exactly as expected.

Diesel fuel (Deliveries)

The forecast uses a factor of £8 per widget, and the variance is showing that the cost was actually 22p more than that. It's quite possible that over the next few months the cumulative variance will move nearer to £8; if it doesn't, then a revised factor should be entered for the remainder of the year. Nothing to worry about yet though.

Wages (Temporary staff)

The forecast uses a factor of £15 per widget; the variance for January was £1.91 less. Again, two or three more months' figures are probably required to get a settled trend and average. Leave the forecast factor as it is for now, but keep an eye on it.

Right, that's all of the revenue and expense variances looked at, but what about profitability?

Profitability

One month of actual data isn't really sufficient to get a meaningful picture, but we'll take a look anyway. Remember there was a new engine for a delivery vehicle that is part of constant direct costs, so we would expect both gross and net profit to have been affected by it. Figure 9.12 shows the profit section of the budget forecast with the actual figures for January, and Figure 9.13 shows the same section before the actual figures for January were entered.

6		Jan	Feb	Mar	Apr
72					
73	**Profitability**				
74	(Excluding capital and start up)				
75					
76	Revenue from sales	93,450	95,000	95,000	95,000
77	Direct costs - Widgets Mk 1	43,940	42,150	42,350	41,900
78	Direct costs - Widgets Mk 2	29,820	30,150	30,350	29,900
79	Gross profit	19,690	22,700	22,300	23,200
80	Gross profit as % of sales	21.1%	23.9%	23.5%	24.4%
81					
82	Overhead costs	18,235	18,700	18,375	18,575
83	Total costs	91,995	91,000	91,075	90,375
84	Net profit	1,455	4,000	3,925	4,625
85	Net profit as % of sales	1.6%	4.2%	4.1%	4.9%
86					
87	**By Product**				
88	Widgets Mk1 - gross profit	12,710	12,850	12,650	13,100
89	as % of sales	22.4%	23.4%	23.0%	23.8%
90					
91	Widgets Mk2 - gross profit	6,980	9,850	9,650	10,100
92	as % of sales	19.0%	24.6%	24.1%	25.3%
93					

Figure 9.12 Profitability section with actual figures for January entered

6		Jan	Feb	Mar	Apr
72					
73	**Profitability**				
74	(Excluding capital and start up)				
75					
76	Revenue from sales	95,000	95,000	95,000	95,000
77	Direct costs - Widgets Mk 1	41,900	42,150	42,350	41,900
78	Direct costs - Widgets Mk 2	29,900	30,150	30,350	29,900
79	Gross profit	23,200	22,700	22,300	23,200
80	Gross profit as % of sales	24.4%	23.9%	23.5%	24.4%
81					
82	Overhead costs	18,575	18,700	18,375	18,575
83	Total costs	90,375	91,000	91,075	90,375
84	Net profit	4,625	4,000	3,925	4,625
85	Net profit as % of sales	4.9%	4.2%	4.1%	4.9%
86					
87	**By Product**				
88	Widgets Mk1 - gross profit	13,100	12,850	12,650	13,100
89	as % of sales	23.8%	23.4%	23.0%	23.8%
90					
91	Widgets Mk2 - gross profit	10,100	9,850	9,650	10,100
92	as % of sales	25.3%	24.6%	24.1%	25.3%
93					

Figure 9.13 Profitability section before actual figures for January were entered

Yes, well spotted, we're about 3 per cent off Gross profits compared to the original. In the 'By Product' section Widgets Mk1 gross profit is 1 per cent lower, and Widgets Mk2 is 6 per cent down.

The reason for this can be seen from looking at the models. The constant direct costs (remember the new van engine) are shared equally between Mk1s and Mk2s and has indeed reduced the gross profit of both. But, Mk2 sales in January were down by 8 and Mk1 sales were up by 6, and of course the lower Mk2 sales have still absorbed 50 per cent of the constant direct costs, which have thus had a proportionally greater impact on gross profit

Cash flow

Now for a look at the impact of the January figures on cash flow. Remember that we have only entered *invoice* figures, not payments or receipts, and so the cash flow forecast will *not necessarily be reflecting actual cash flow*. To obtain that, we must get the *payment* figures for January and enter them. More of that later – for now we'll look at the effect so far. Figure 9.14 shows the variance section of the cash flow forecast after the entry of actual January data in the sales and budget forecasts.

⤳ brilliant reminder

Remember – this is the difference between the original forecast, and the impact of the January invoice details in the sales and budget forecasts.

107	VARIANCES (Actual – Fixed Original)					
108						
109	CASH FLOW AND BANK					
110						
111	Net cash flow	(3,610)	(1,600)			
112						
113	Balance B/F		(3,610)	(5,210)	(5,210)	(5,210)
114	Cash In	(1,550)	(1,550)			
115	Cash Out	2,060	50			
116	Balance C/F	(3,610)	(5,210)	(5,210)	(5,210)	(5,210)

Figure 9.14 The variance section of the cash forecast

Net cash flow

In January a total of £3,610 less net cash has flown through the business. Net cash flow is the sum of *cash in* and *cash out*.

Balance B/F

As this is the first month, there will be no change to the balance brought forward.

Cash in

£1,550 less cash came into the business than forecast.

Cash out

£2,060 more cash went out of the business than forecast.

Balance C/F

The balance carried forward is different to the forecast by the same amount as the Net Cash Flow + Balance B/F variances.

And there is really little else to be said about the cash flow. As long as it remains wholly dependent upon the budget forecast, then the impact on it will be driven entirely by the offset of the links between them. But remember that it is *not* a literal representation of cash flow, only notional based on the offsets.

If a true picture of cash flow is needed, then the actual *payment* figures (meaning cash payments and receipts) must be entered in the cash flow operational block, overwriting the link formulae to the budget.

⟳ brilliant reminder

Don't forget, the actual figures must be exclusive of VAT.

The method is exactly the same as for the budget, and there is no need to repeat it. However, if actual payment and receipt figures are going to be put in, then another facility becomes available from the system – the calculation of accruals and prepayments.

◈ brilliant definition

An *expense accrual* is the amount of money owed, but not yet paid, for goods or services already received.

A *sales accrual* is the amount of money owed, but not yet received, for goods or services already supplied to a customer.

Providing that actual cash flow details have been entered, the forecasting and monitoring system contains all of the information required to calculate how accruals stand, or will stand, in any period.

To calculate expense accruals to any given period:

Total budget forecast costs to the period –
Total cash flow forecast payments to the period

their difference is what has yet to be paid.

Look at this expense accrual example:

	Jan	Feb	Mar	Apr	£ Total
Budget cost	500	200	300	400	**1400**
Cash paid	300	100	200	500	**1100**

Expense accruals at April = £1,400 – £1,100 = £300

To calculate sales accruals to any given period:

Total budget forecast sales to the period –
Total cash flow forecast receipts to the period

their difference is what has yet to be received.

Look at this sales accrual example:

	Jan	Feb	Mar	Apr	£ Total
Budget sales	2000	3000	2500	3000	**10500**
Cash received	1500	2500	3000	2000	**9000**

Sales accruals at April = £10,500 – £9,000 = £1,500

Finally, the current assets of the company can be calculated for the period end simply by:

Balance C/F + Sales accruals – Expense accruals

It doesn't matter if either expense or sales accruals are negative values, the sum still works out.

brilliant definition

A negative value expense accrual is sometimes called a *purchase prepayment*; it means that cash has been paid before goods or services have been received.

A negative value sales accrual is sometimes called a *sales prepayment*; it means that cash has been received in advance of supplying goods or services.

Summary

In this chapter we have:

- allocated the budget using the principle of a single budget available to everyone who needs to know, and stressed the objective of simplicity;
- discussed three viable methods of retaining a copy of the original budget, and we chose a combination of 'paper' and 'key figure copy' for Widget Makers Ltd;
- entered actual 'invoice' figures for January in the sales and budget forecasts, and examined the results;
- discussed the impact of the January actual figures on the cash flow, and we saw that entry of actual 'payment' figures into the cash flow is identical, in principle, to that for the budget;
- explored the concept of accruals, and we saw that budget and cash flow forecasts together provide all information necessary for their calculation.

CHAPTER 10

Further analysis

This chapter is about ...

Looking in more depth at the impact of changes on cash flow, such as sales volume peaks, smooth growth and how a profitable business can run out of cash.

The impact of change on cash flow

The budget forecast we set up for Widget Makers Ltd has a flat sales profile – the same volume of sales for each month of the year. This is not of course realistic; most businesses experience volume changes of some sort: they may just be fluctuations above and below a steady annual average, increases through growth, decreases through falling business, or perhaps seasonal variations. Or, during the forecast's span, a combination of all of them.

When all of these factors are operating together the resulting effect on cash flow is quite complex and certainly difficult to visualise. The combined effects could of course be described in detail, but you wouldn't thank me for it, it's far better just to produce a graph that shows the relevant figures. However, the basic principles operating to create the effects are very simple indeed and well worth looking at.

We can use the original Widget Makers Ltd forecast, but only need to consider the figures directly affected:

- sales volume (total);
- cash in (from sales);
- cash out for widget parts.

By looking initially at just these figures, we won't confuse the principles with the overlaid effects of everything else in the budget forecast.

This is how the timing offsets of Cash in and Cash out are related to sales for Widget Makers Ltd over May, June and July for example:

	May	*June*	*July*
Cash out for widget parts	XX		
Sales		XX	
Cash in			XX

Cash is paid out for widget parts one month before the sale is shown in the forecast, and cash is received in from the sales one month after.

I have set up a graph in the cash flow forecast that shows just the relevant figures. The sales volumes are plotted on the right-hand y-axis.

Flat sales profile

Figure 10.1 shows the forecast for the original flat sales volumes. Note that 'Minimum balance' and 'Annual net cash flow' are still shown, and their values are of course the same as when the budget was first compiled in Figure 7.5.

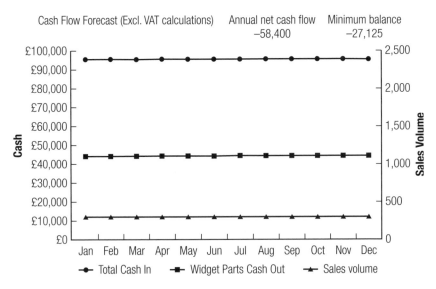

Figure 10.1 Flat sales profile

Sales volume peaks

To illustrate the effect of volume changes, we'll first of all put an increase in just one month, from 200 to 1,000 Widgets Mk1 in June. The increase of 800 Widgets Mk1 is perhaps unrealistically large, but it helps to highlight the effect. Figure 10.2a shows what happens, and you can see clearly that the *cash out* peak is occurring one month before the additional sales, and the *cash in* for them one month later.

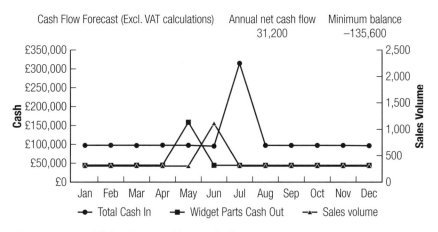

Figure 10.2a Additional 800 Widgets Mk1 in June

Also, look at the Annual net cash flow in Figure 10.2b. It's now a healthy positive number as a result of the large June sales. But the minimum balance has dropped through the floor from −£27,127 in Figure 7.5 to −£135,600!

A thousand sales of Widgets Mk1 in June, better annual net cash flow: how can the minimum bank balance have fallen to that level? It's because the parts for the additional 800 Widgets Mk1 in June had to be paid for in May. We'll look more closely at this effect a little later.

Some businesses may experience large 'one-off' peaks of sales, others will have more gradual changes.

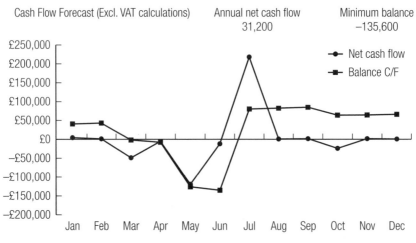

Figure 10.2b Additional 800 Widgets Mk1 in June – cash forecast

Smooth sales growth

Figure 10.3 shows the effect of smooth sales volume growth of Widgets Mkl from January to June, and reversion to the original monthly volumes from July onwards.

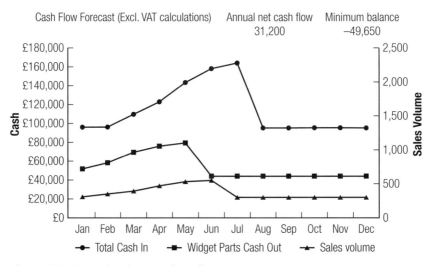

Figure 10.3 Smooth sales growth until June

The growth from January to June has been deliberately set so that the total widgets sold in the year is the same as in the previous single increase example.

Jan	Feb	Mar	Apr	May	Jun	Jul	Aug
200	250	300	375	425	450	200	200

In this case, Annual net cash flow is very similar to the single increase example, but the minimum balance has improved considerably. Yet the total sales, and hence *profit, in both cases is about the same.*

This shows how different profiles of the same levels of sales can have markedly different effects on cash flow.

The overall effect of sales volume changes on cash flow

Now, having examined the principles, let's look again at the whole picture with respect to cash flow for each version of the additional 800 sales.

Figure 10.4 shows the single increase and Figure 10.5 the smooth growth from January until June. (Note that the figures have different scales.)

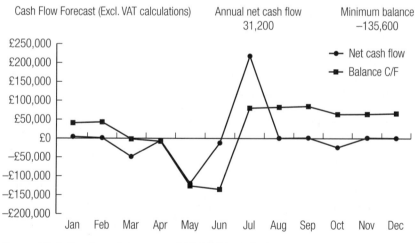

Figure 10.4 Single peak increase of 800 Widgets in June

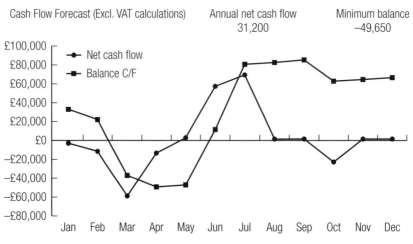

Figure 10.5 Smooth growth increase of 800 Widgets

If this were a real bank account, the year end balance for the single increase version would be lower than for the smooth increase version, because of higher overdraft charges. Clearly it would be a good idea to add a bank overdraft interest calculation to the cash flow forecast in a case like this.

Earlier and later sales receipts

In Chapter 8 we saw the impact of overhead payment timing changes on cash flow. The effect of timing changes on sales volume related items would be very similar to those on overheads for a flat sales profile, but conspicuously different when applied to a growth profile.

Earlier cash payments or later sales receipts will very significantly worsen cash flow, and conversely, later cash payments or earlier sales receipts will significantly improve it.

We'll just use earlier and later sales receipts, on the same January to June growth in the previous example, to illustrate the principle.

Earlier

Figure 10.6 shows the effect of one month earlier sales receipts. Whilst Annual net cash flow is unaffected because the growth is only in the first part of the year, the minimum balance has improved by about £40,000 to just over –£9,000.

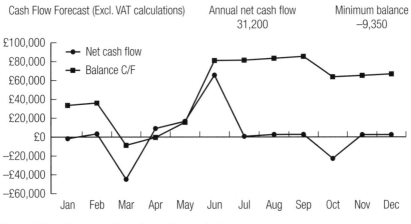

Figure 10.6 One month earlier sales receipts

Figure 10.7 shows the effect of one month later sales receipts. Again, Annual net cash flow is not affected (another dummy figure had to be put into February Cash in), the minimum balance has worsened by about £45,000 to –£95,000. Again, this would have very severe implications for interest charges in a bank account.

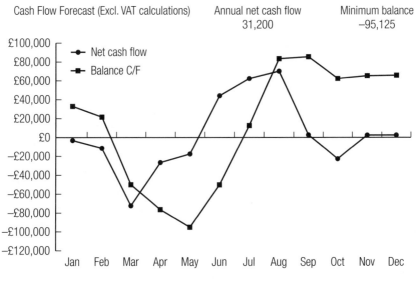

Figure 10.7 One month later sales receipts

The effect of rapid growth on cash flow

Finally, in this section, we'll have a look at the effect of growth to the point where cash flow goes into 'reverse', and the bank balance gets worse month by month, although the business is in fact still profitable.

This effect is driven by a volume growth steep enough that the cash received for earlier sales is insufficient to cover the direct costs – that must be paid for in advance for the greater quantity of sales orders ahead – after constant and overhead expenses have been paid.

The level of growth required to cause reverse cash flow is a combined function of, and the relationship between:

- cost of direct variables;
- timing of payment for direct variable costs;
- net profit;
- overheads;
- timing of sales receipts.

Generally, the conditions susceptible to reverse cash flow are low net profit margins, variable direct costs, a high proportion of total direct costs, small overheads compared to total costs, and high *debtor days* (the time taken for sales invoices to be paid).

In Figure 10.8, rather than meddle with Widget Makers' fairly comfortable circumstances, which aren't especially susceptible to reverse cash flow, I've introduced a rather impracticably high sales growth to illustrate the effect. This also shows that even a comfortable business cannot afford to be complacent if faced with an opportunity for rapid growth.

The growth is 50 per cent month on month, for Widgets Mk1 and Mk2, from February through to September, after which the volumes are restored to their starting values of 300 widgets total per month. Cutting off growth in September illustrates the extraordinary effect as the tidal wave of cash owed to the business floods in.

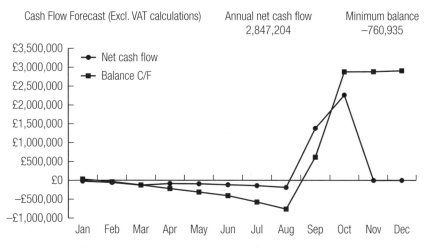

Figure 10.8 Fifty per cent month-on-month growth from February to September

Tell the bank what's happening

A major reason to understand this effect is so that a coherent reason to borrow money, in this case more than three-quarters of a million pounds (see the minimum balance), can be presented to the fund provider, usually a bank. You must show the bank that although your borrowing requirements are increasing rapidly, the reason is profitable growth. A bank manager who is not informed about what is happening is just as likely to regard a rising overdraft as indicative of the business's poor profitability, assuming they look at the statements and see the sales receipts on them, or as a declining business, if they don't.

brilliant tip

Make sure your provider of cash funding understands what is happening in the business.

'What if' analysis

Often a forecast will be created solely for the purpose of testing various business plans, strategic policies and so on. Because such a forecast will not be used for budgetary allocation and control, its format and content can be arranged in any way to suit the purpose.

Nevertheless, a purpose-built budget forecast can also be used for 'what if' analysis. We have already carried out quite a bit for Widget Makers Ltd – what if sales growth increased dramatically? what if capital expenditure was deferred, or brought forward? – and so on.

brilliant tip

The most important thing to remember in 'what-if'ing is that it will only generate realistic predictions if all of the significant factors that impact on it are built into the model. For instance, if an item of expense that is significantly dependent upon sales volumes isn't in fact linked to them, then clearly the wrong answer will be obtained when the volumes are changed.

But, if sales volumes are not going to be altered in a 'what if' scenario, then no linking to them is needed at all.

The danger lies in building a model for a very specific purpose in which, for the sake of simplicity, no unnecessary relationships and links have been included, but later on using the model for a different purpose in which those links are essential.

Summary

In this chapter we have:

- looked at the effect of the time relationships between sales, variable direct cost cash payments, and cash in from sales on cash flow;
- seen that for Widget Makers Ltd a smooth growth to achieve increased sales placed less burden on cash resources than a single sales peak;
- seen the timing of cash payments and receipts is a most significant factor of cash flow quality;
- understood reverse cash flow, and seen it illustrated in Widget Makers Ltd with a 50 per cent month-on-month sales growth;
- met the principles of 'what if' analysis.

PART 5

Handling VAT

Value Added Tax (VAT) is something that all but the smallest of businesses must be concerned with. However, it may not be necessary for every budget controller and forecaster to take account of it, especially in departmental budgets.

As a rule of thumb:

- if the forecast is at the highest level of the business, and if it includes a cash flow forecast that is intended to represent the reality of cash movements, then accounting for VAT is essential;
- if a cash flow forecast at any level in the business is intended to be a notional representation of cash movements only (see Chapter 9) then accounting for VAT is unnecessary.

VAT can only be dealt with if there is a cash flow forecast and a budget forecast. So if a budget model does not have a cash flow forecast, VAT can be ignored entirely.

Important: While the concept of VAT and the way in which it is handled in a cash flow forecast is simple and straightforward, the detailed rules applied by HM Revenue & Customs are many, and in some instances very complex. Interpretation and application of the rules is, therefore, best done with the help of a qualified professional.

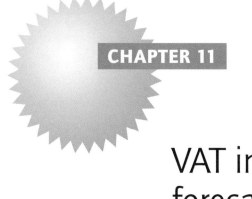

CHAPTER 11

VAT in the forecast

This chapter is about ...

What VAT (Value Added Tax) is and how it works. We'll then add calculations for VAT to the illustration framework and see how it affects forecast cash flow.

What is VAT?

brilliant definition

VAT is a tax, administered by HM Revenue & Customs (HMRC) in the UK, which every business with a turnover greater than a certain limit must add on to the selling price of its products or services. A business with a turnover greater than the limit *must* be registered for VAT with HMRC; but businesses with a lower turnover may apply for voluntary registration.

A business not registered for VAT must *not* add the tax to its charges – this is illegal.

At intervals, usually quarterly, the VAT charged to customers is sent on to HMRC. This payment, and the form associated with it, are known as the VAT return.

Businesses that are registered for VAT pay the tax on their own purchases, but reclaim it from HMRC. The reclamation is not a separate process, but part of the VAT return. On the return form, the amount being reclaimed is subtracted from the amount due from sales, and the balance then sent to HMRC. If the amount claimed is greater than the amount due from sales, the return is still made and HMRC refunds the difference to the business – see Figure 11.1.

Example 1: VAT payment

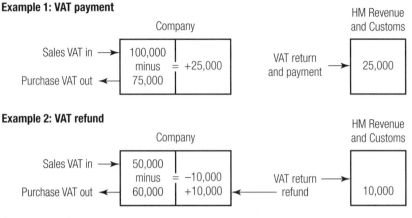

Figure 11.1 The VAT return

Calculating and paying VAT

The VAT for a quarter is based on either invoices or cash transactions. Larger businesses must base their return on invoices, but smaller ones may apply for it to be related to cash movements.

Invoice accounting for VAT

To calculate VAT due to HMRC, the VAT components of sales with an invoice date within the quarter are added up, then the VAT components of purchases with an invoice date within the quarter are added up and subtracted from the sales VAT sum.

The difference is then paid to (or refunded by) HMRC.

Cash accounting for VAT

To calculate VAT due to HMRC, the VAT components of sales cash received within the quarter are added up, then the VAT components of cash paid out for purchases within the quarter are added up and subtracted from the sales VAT sum.

The difference is then paid to (or refunded by) HMRC.

VAT payment

The VAT return and payment fall due on the last day of the month following the quarter end. Thus if a VAT quarter is April to June, the last invoices or transactions included in the return for the period will occur on 30 June, and the return must be sent off to be received by HMRC by 31 July.

brilliant tip

Great care must be taken when completing a VAT return and ensuring it is sent off before the deadline. Errors and late payments, even one day, are liable to financial penalties. On the other hand, sending the payment earlier than necessary can have a significant effect on cash flow if the quarter was profitable.

Take a profitable quarter, as in Example 1 in Figure 11.1. The £25,000 has been accumulating in the bank over the quarter, either offsetting borrowing charges or earning interest. If the VAT return is completed and despatched with the payment of £25,000 early in July, then nearly one month of its benefit to your bank account is lost. *But don't be late either!*

In an unprofitable quarter, as in Example 2 of Figure 11.1, the £10,000 due as a refund has been lost from the bank over the quarter, and the sooner the return is despatched after 30 June the sooner the refund will be obtained and the sooner your bank account will benefit from it. *But don't rush it and create errors either!*

VAT calculations

Our calculations here are based on *VAT invoice accounting*. The *cash accounting* method will be outlined afterwards. There are four stages to calculating VAT:

1 The amounts due on sales and purchase invoices are calculated in the budget/P&L forecast. (Remember – VAT under the invoice accounting scheme is based on sales and purchase invoices, and when they occur is in the budget forecast.)

2 Then, the amount of VAT paid and received through the bank in the normal course of business is accounted for in the cash flow forecast.

3 Then, the amount due to, or from, HMRC each quarter is calculated in the budget forecast.

4 Finally, the amount paid to, or received from, HMRC is accounted for in the cash flow forecast.

Not all purchases and sales are subject to VAT. In this example there are some purchases (rent and business rates for instance) that are not subject to VAT, but the assumption is made that *all* sales are subject to VAT.

In schematic form, this is what the spreadsheet models need to do:

Stages

Budget forecast	*Cash flow forecast*
(1) Calculate sales VAT due	VAT Cash in (2)
(1) Calculate purchase VAT due	VAT Cash out (2)
(3) Calculate VAT return —— link ——▶	VAT return (4)

We'll start by putting the calculations for stages (1) and (3) into the budget forecast.

> **Note:** The VAT calculations are already included in Completed Illustration Framework.xls.

Budget VAT calculations

There is a convenient block of spare rows in the budget just below the profit calculations for you to enter the row headings and formulae shown in Figure 11.2. Note that only formulae for columns B and E are shown, i.e. for January and April.

	A	B	E
96	Enter VAT rate (%) >>	17.5	
97			
98	Expenses subject to VAT	=B69-(B41+B49+B58+B59+B60)	=E69-(E41+E49+E58+E59+E60)
99			
100	VAT due on purchases	B98*$VATRATE	E98*$VATRATE
101			
102	VAT due from sales	B16*$VATRATE	E16*$VATRATE
103			
104	Net VAT / month	B102-B100	E102-E100
105			
106	VAT return to HMRC	E106	SUM(B102:D102) – SUM(B100:D100)

Figure 11.2 Budget forecast VAT calculations

Notes to Figure 11.2

1 Cell B96 provides the facility to enter the VAT rate, so that it can be easily changed if the rate alters. I have given B96 the name VATRATE.

2 The expenses subject to VAT are most easily calculated by subtracting from the total cost (row 69) all expenses that are not subject to VAT, which are:

Wages (Temporary staff)
Salaries (Widget production)
Postage
Rates
Salaries

3 VAT due on purchases, and from sales, is calculated by multiplying them by the VAT rate.

4 Net VAT/month is sales VAT less expenses VAT.

5 Using VAT quarter periods of:

Jan – Mar
Apr – Jun
Jul – Sep
Oct – Dec

then the VAT return is due in the month following the end of each period, so April, July, October and January of the following year. Using the formulae shown for April (column E) subtract the VAT due on purchases from the VAT due from sales in January to March. Replicate the formulae for July and October. Because we do not have a forecast for the previous year, a dummy VAT return figure has been entered in January by picking up the figure from the next return in April (E106).

Figure 11.3 shows the VAT calculations for the whole year. Note that the Net VAT/month for March is negative, because the VAT on purchases is greater than for sales in that month.

	A	B	C	D	E	F	G	H	I	J	K	L	M	N
96	Enter VAT rate (%) >> 17.5													
97														
98	Expenses subject to VAT	48,585	49,410	99,485	58,585	58,910	51,285	50,585	51,410	50,785	75,585	51,410	51,285	697,320
99														
100	VAT due on purchases	8,502	8,647	17,410	10,252	10,309	8,975	8,852	8,997	8,887	13,227	8,997	8,975	122,031
101														
102	VAT due from sales	16,625	16,625	16,625	16,625	16,625	16,625	16,625	16,625	16,625	16,625	16,625	16,625	199,500
103														
104	Net VAT / month	8,123	7,978	–785	6,373	6,316	7,650	7,773	7,628	7,738	3,398	7,628	7,650	
105														
106	VAT return to HMRC	15,316			15,316			20,339			23,139			

Figure 11.3 VAT calculated in the budget forecast

Cash flow forecast VAT calculations

Now we look at the calculations for stages (2) and (4) in the cash flow forecast.

There is a convenient block of spare rows in the cash flow forecast, 74–85, just below the key indicators for you to enter the row headings and formulae shown in Figure 11.4.

	A	B
74	VAT rate (%)=VATRATE	
75		
76	Payments subject to VAT	=B57-(B29+B37+B46+B47+B48)
77		
78	VAT paid	B76*$VATRATE
79	VAT received	B12*$VATRATE
80	Net VAT flow	B79-B78
81		
82	VAT return to HMRC	='Budget Forecast'!B106
83		
84	Net cash flow (With VAT included)	=B12-B57+B80-B82
85	Balance C/F (VAT calculated)	=B66+B80-B82

Figure 11.4 Cash flow forecast VAT calculations

Notes to Figure 11.4

1 Cell B74 picks up the VAT named range VATRATE from the budget forecast.

2 The payments subject to VAT are most easily calculated by subtracting from the total cash out (row 57) all cash out not subject to VAT, which are: Wages (Temporary staff); Salaries (Widget production); Postage; Rates; Salaries.

3 VAT paid and received is calculated by multiplying by the VAT rate.

4 Net VAT flow is VAT received less VAT paid.

5 The VAT return to HMRC is picked up from the budget forecast.

6 Balance C/F (VAT calculated) adds the VAT flow and subtracts the VAT return.

Figure 11.5 shows the VAT flow and resulting bank balance for the year.

	A	B	C	D	E	F	G	H	I	J	K	L	M	N
74	VAT rate (%) 17.5													
75														
76	Payments subject to VAT	48,585	49,410	99,485	58,585	58,910	51,285	50,585	51,410	50,785	75,585	51,410	51,285	697,320
77														
78	VAT paid	8,502	8,647	17,410	10,252	10,309	8,975	8,852	8,997	8,887	13,227	8,997	8,975	122,031
79	VAT received	16,625	16,625	16,625	16,625	16,625	16,625	16,625	16,625	16,625	16,625	16,625	16,625	199,500
80	Net VAT flow	8,123	7,978	-785	6,373	6,316	7,650	7,773	7,628	7,738	3,398	7,628	7,650	77,469
81														
82	VAT return to HMRC	15,316	0	0	15,316	0	0	20,339	0	0	23,139	0	0	0
83														
84	Net cash flow (With VAT included)	-2,568	11,978	-46,860	-14,318	616	9,575	-9,941	9,428	10,163	-42,116	9,428	9,575	**-55,040**
85	Balance C/F (VAT calculated)	32,432	51,603	-3,235	-16,768	-7,209	-3,950	-21,541	453	2,988	-46,866	-17,697	-15,750	77,469

Figure 11.5 VAT calculated in the cash flow forecast

Closing balances compared

Now that VAT calculations have been added, the resulting balance carried forward will usually be higher than before in non-VAT return months. This is because although the VAT paid out on purchases (an average of £10,169/month) has been taken from the cash flow, this is more than offset on a monthly basis by the VAT received (an average of £16,625/month). In VAT return months though, when the VAT due to HMRC is paid, the closing balance will usually be lower.

Figure 11.6 shows the original Balance C/F together with the version that includes the VAT flow.

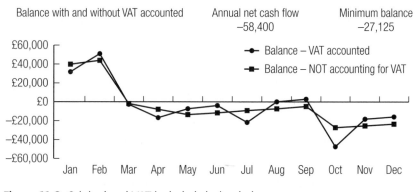

Figure 11.6 Original and VAT included closing balances

And that completes the calculations for VAT invoice accounting.

VAT cash accounting

brilliant definition

The principles of constructing VAT calculations under the cash accounting scheme are almost the same as for the invoice scheme. There is only one difference: the VAT return to HMRC is not based on the invoice values in the budget, but on the cash paid and received in the cash flow.

So, to convert what has already been built into a cash accounting version:

1 In the budget forecast, delete the row (106) that calculates the VAT return.

2 In the cash flow forecast, in row (82) headed 'VAT return to HMRC', replace the links to the budget forecast with formulae in the VAT payment months (April, July, October – and January from the previous year) that sum the Net VAT flow for the previous three months.

3 So in April (column E, row 82) enter **=SUM(B80:D80)**.

4 In July (column H, row 82) enter **=SUM(E80:G80)**.

5 In October (column K, row 82) enter **=SUM(H80:J80)**.

6 For illustration purposes January can use a dummy figure from the next quarter April, so in B82 enter **=D82**.

And that's that!

Monitoring and reviewing

The methods we've already seen for monitoring and reviewing are the same with or without VAT calculations, but remember that only actuals entered in the budget forecast will be picked up for the VAT return calculation. In other words, the rule about putting actuals into the lowest point in the dependency hierarchy still applies.

Summary

In this chapter we have:

- understood the concept of Value Added Tax (VAT);
- seen that VAT calculations *must* be included if the cash flow forecast is intended to present a realistic view of the company's bank account;
- looked at the principle of the quarterly VAT return, and the importance of its timing for cash flow was demonstrated;
- added VAT calculations for invoice accounting to the budget and cash flow forecasts;
- seen that accounting for VAT usually means a gradually improving bank balance between VAT returns, as compared with the balance when VAT is not accounted for;
- looked at the minor modifications needed to convert the models to VAT cash accounting.

PART 6

Measuring and controlling costs

In this part we'll first be looking at ways of measuring and controlling costs, including the introduction of a powerful technique known as Activity Based Costing (ABC) or revenue cost analysis.

CHAPTER 12

Measuring and controlling costs

This chapter is about ...

Measuring and controlling production and manpower costs. We'll look at where to start, and ideas for reducing costs, especially general overheads. Also we'll look in detail at a practical way to find out where all that manpower time goes, from allocation through to recording and analysing. Importantly for some we'll also see how to deal with doubters – those who oppose the rationale for measuring where time goes.

First things first

To be able to control costs you need to know what they are – a statement of the obvious if ever there was one! To be sure, the degree of cost breakdown that we've looked at so far will, for some businesses, be all that is required. However, for many businesses a greater level of breakdown – and perhaps a different approach – will give a lot more insight and enable a greater degree of cost management.

brilliant tip

Measuring and controlling costs is principally about improving profitability, which in turn will improve cash flow of course.

The way in which direct costs are approached and controlled can be quite different to the methods used for overhead costs. But, as we've seen, some businesses might not have identified any specific direct costs and simply put everything into an overhead category. Now, for some businesses this might be the only sensible way for them: a one man business in the service sector that has only one identifiable 'product' or stream of revenue might not have any costs directly attributable to the product or volume of sales. However, for the same one man business selling a number of different services, each with its own revenue stream, it might be a very different matter, and be quite possible to identify the particular costs associated with the delivery of specific services.

In any event, there is an approach known as Activity Based Costing (ABC) which effectively disregards whether a cost is initially categorised as direct or overhead. First though we'll look at the basics of measuring and managing traditional direct and overhead costs as used in the Illustration Framework spreadsheets.

Absolute figures and percentages

Whereas the absolute figures for costs and revenues are what ultimately drive profitability, the proportion or percentage represented by each are often the key to determining where and how to make improvements.

In the budget/P&L forecast of the Illustration Framework there are formulae to the right of the year totals that calculate the percentage each cost row represents of the total in its block, for example each overhead row as a percentage of the total overhead cost.

Which costs should we start with?

In any cost structure there are items that are more straightforward to address than others, and usually some that are a significantly greater proportion of the total. These are the ones to start with. If you're lucky, some of the straightforward ones might also be amongst the more significant.

By 'straightforward' I mean those that are simple in structure, usually purchases such as bought in goods and services, telephone charges, stationery, printing for example, or perhaps raw materials or bought in components.

The less straightforward costs are likely to be those directly related to production and delivery, especially those associated with manpower salary costs, and particularly the manpower costs within a service business rather than one engaged in manufacturing.

We'll look at purchasing costs overall, and then at production and manpower costs with particular emphasis on *service-based businesses*.

Purchases

Remember we are looking first at those costs that are among the higher proportion of total costs. There are two main lines of attack:

- the amount of consumption within the business, and
- the costs from suppliers.

Consumption

Consumption is a difficult factor for me to give generalised guidance on as much depends upon each business's own circumstances. For variable direct costs, consumption is obviously dictated by production volume. This isn't by any means to say that a reduction in consumption isn't possible of course – for example, costs of delivery or, in the case of manufacturing, the amount of raw materials wastage can be looked at – but whilst variable direct costs might well be productive areas for review each business will have its own very particular details. But here are some tips that may help.

brilliant tip

- **Habit and convention** – over time we develop ways of working which become taken for granted. It is well worth asking 'Why do we do it that way?' and checking that the reasons are still valid. If one of the more significant costs is being reviewed it will almost always be worthwhile looking very carefully at established practices, processes and procedures for efficiency and cost savings.

- **Cut off the supply** – how can we possibly be using that many/that amount of... just about anything? All too frequently the answer is justified by all manner of arguments. Now, you could set up a relatively time consuming exercise to find out exactly how it's all being used, or you could just severely restrict or even entirely cut supply of the item in question. OK, this needs some common sense to avoid damaging the business, but you'll be amazed at what you find out, how well people cope, and how much you can save. There should be no danger to staff morale if you keep them informed and take them with you. Explain why the costs of running the business are being looked at and how any improvements will be good for them too.

- **Storerooms and cupboards** – might contain far more supplies than are needed, in other words it isn't all being consumed but is just being piled up. Repetitive ordering is often at the root of this – every month or quarter the same order is placed, with no account taken of how much has been used and by whom.

Costs from suppliers

Dealing with these can be very straightforward, especially for items widely available from many sources.

● Get in touch with each of your suppliers and ask for a review of your prices – point out that they haven't been reviewed for x months or years and that you are looking for reductions for loyalty or firm orders.

● Obtain prices from other suppliers and tell your current supplier who has given you a lower price.

● Offer earlier payment in return for a price reduction.

● Ask if they can offer a suitable lower cost alternative.

● As with consumption, watch out for habitual purchasing, i.e. things that have become custom and practice over a period of time.

brilliant tip

Often it's always the same person who orders certain supplies. Give them a target for reducing the cost – just the objective, not how to do it. Again you could be pleasantly surprised at the gusto with which people will attack it: it becomes a personal challenge so give them their head.

Measuring production costs

Production purchase costs

Production costs are those we have called variable direct and constant direct – they are directly related to the production of the good or service. As we've seen, the variable direct costs are those that reflect production volumes, rising and falling in a fixed arithmetic relationship. Constant direct costs are there as a cost of production, but are far less likely in a normal production pattern to be affected by rising and falling volumes.

We have already looked at the relatively straightforward matters of consumption and purchasing prices, but how about the matter of apportioning costs across a range of products or services? This is less a matter of managing consumption or purchase prices, but rather about understanding the whole cost structure of a product or service to enable the profitability and viability of each to be assessed.

For variable direct costs it's usually clear cut: if Item A is only used for one good or service in the range, or even if Item B is used for a number of the products, then it's probably quite straightforward to show how many are used for each product.

In the case of constant direct costs it is much less straightforward. Indeed, the fact that a cost has been categorised as a constant direct immediately implies that there is some difficulty in apportioning it across the product range – otherwise it would have been regarded as a variable direct cost. Consider say the heating, lighting and electrical power costs of the production area. We could apportion these according to the floor space each product occupies, by volume of production, value of sales, or by all three – or maybe some other factor. Any of these or another factor may be entirely valid, or sufficient for the purpose.

brilliant tip

It's important to keep things in proportion, and not expend a large amount of effort in trying to refine the apportionment of costs unless there's going to be a significant benefit. If a good approximation provides all the detail that's needed – fine.

However, in more complex cases and if there is a significant advantage of being able to measure individual product costs, then activity based costing might be worth considering. We'll look at that after taking a look at manpower costs.

Measuring manpower costs

Manpower costs associated with variable direct activities might already be well understood and measured. They are usually straightforward to measure and, what's more, commercial imperatives dictate that you should do so. But the manpower costs associated with constant direct and overhead activities are often overlooked, particularly in service and support organisations, including public sector organisations such as central government departments and local authorities.

In these types of organisations salary costs are often by far the most significant, but despite this they are often virtually ignored. Why is this? Maybe it's because they don't change from month to month and so don't appear in an analysis of variations. Perhaps there's simply a culture of 'that's what they are and there's nothing that can be done about them' – but in my experience nothing could be further from the truth. Except for the smallest of businesses, say five employees or less, unless a procedure along the lines of what follows is being carried out I can almost guarantee that at least modest savings, and in many case significant ones, can be made.

The next section on activity based costing outlines a rigorous method of assessing costs across the board, but it does take a fair bit of effort. In most cases nowhere as much effort is required to still have a major impact on costs. So how is it done without too much effort? First of all you need the unshakeable conviction that it is at least worth trying. More to the point, if there's a solid business imperative underlying the need to address overhead manpower costs then you're most of the way there – you really can't avoid dealing with it.

Doubters

There will probably be doubters among your colleagues – suggestions that just doing a little of it for a couple of weeks will give you the information you need. Not so. It needs to be done properly and continuously, a 'special exercise' every now and then just won't work.

'We need more people – not fewer!' Of course there are circumstances where that could be the case, for example and simplistically if there is more *profitable* business than can be handled with the current work force. But I have also heard this argument where it is by no means certain that having more people will create an increase in profitable business. The counter argument for these and other doubters is straightforward, unambiguous, solid and inescapable. Simply – let's find out, it'll take very little effort to make the case one way or the other, and we'll at least have measurable facts to base decisions on.

Getting started

The key is to measure what people spend their time on, but to do it in a way that makes both data capture and analysis easy. Whichever way you choose it should only take each individual 5–10 minutes a day to record their activities, and a couple of hours a month to carry out analysis to at least a first level of insight.

brilliant tip

This is important – if the method of information capture isn't easy it won't be done properly.

There may be some resistance at first, probably along the lines of 'it'll take too long, it isn't worth doing, I object to being spied upon, etc...' For most people an explanation of why it is being done will be enough. Explain that you're not trying to account for every minute of the day, and you won't be expecting records to be kept of rest periods or the time spent talking about business generalities.

Allocating time spent

To be able to obtain a meaningful analysis it's obviously important that everyone records their time using a common set of headings. You should have no more headings than are absolutely necessary, and it's far better to start off with too few than too many. You can always add to them as necessary, and the fewer there are the easier it will be to get the recording up and running.

1 You will need a heading for each revenue stream, or groups of revenue streams if you have a large number of them. It needs to be obvious from the names of the headings what they're about – so Product 1, Product 2, etc... won't do; use whatever description is commonly used in the business. In a business with low-volume, high-value sales you'll probably be able to use the client or project name as the heading.

2 Headings will also be needed for any activity that can't be allocated to a revenue stream. For example, marketing activities in relation to the whole business and not to any specific revenue stream, support and

maintenance of office computers, product or service development work that spans more than one revenue stream, general office administration, the accounts department if their activities can't be broken down by revenue stream, etc...

3 Sub-headings might be needed as well, to capture time spent on different activities under one heading. For example, if a revenue stream involves someone travelling, then the time spent on that could probably be usefully captured; time spent working up a new product or service should also be identified.

Although every business is unique and will need its own unique set of headings, the following example might help to illustrate the principles.

brilliant example

This example is for a software company who develop, sell and support their own products. It's a low-volume/high-value sales business with a significant proportion of its revenue coming from support work. This means that customer names can be used for both implementation and support activities.

Table 12.1 Example work-log headings

Heading	Sub-headings	Qualifier (if needed)
Customer name	Implementation	Stage of implementation
	Support	Aspect of the customer's system
Internal	Development	Product or service
	IT support	General or a specific activity
	Sales activity	Prospect name or general
	Cost of quality	What time has been wasted on*
	Administration	Accounts, personnel, etc.

* For example, if some implementation work had to be done again because it wasn't done properly the first time due to a failure of procedure, documentation or whatever, then don't allocate it to customer name but to this heading. You will then be able to see where your work methods need to be improved.

The simple test of whether you've got the right set of headings will be that you can get out of them what you need to know about where employee hours are being spent. But again don't overdo it or you'll have an impractical system that won't be used properly and will be of no value at all.

Recording time spent

Having created a set of headings you now need to get everyone – and I do mean everyone, including and especially you – to record their time. The simplest possible way is for everyone at the end of each day to note down in an email, or using one of the many software packages available for recording hours from which the details can be copied to an email, how much time they've spent on what.

brilliant tip

Make sure it is at the end of every day. If memory is being relied upon to record the time accurately it will often be vague the next day.

If the emails are sent to one person whose job it is to maintain the central record, then no one else will need to remember the exact headings and their sub-headings; the person making the central record will have the experience and knowledge to correctly allocate it.

Alternatively you could set up the central record so that everyone has access to it and enters their times directly. It isn't a difficult thing to do technically, but be aware that:

- The system will have to ensure that only valid entries are made.
- There will have to be a check that everyone has complied.
- There will have to be a check that it's been done properly.

A better solution for a larger company, where it's impractical for one person to compile the central record, is to break the job down into departments or manageable sized groups and make one person responsible for recording. These departmental records can then easily be added to the central record.

The central and departmental records can most easily be created using Excel – it's very easy to set up, data is easy to enter, it's easy to add departmental records to the central version, and there are more than enough database tools within Excel for the analysis. Of course any database could be used, Access for example, but that will require more specialist skills.

brilliant example

Here are a couple of rows of the central work-log record in Excel for the example company above.

Table 12.2 Structure of an example central work-log record

Date	Who	Heading	Sub heading	Qualifier	Hours
dd-mm-yy	F. Smith	Project 1	Implementation	Stage 3	4.5
dd-mm-yy	B. Jones	Internal	Development	Product B	5.25

Analysis

Within just a couple of weeks you will start to have enough information to be able to make some meaningful analysis. More importantly, and as time goes on, there will be enough data to inform changes that need to be made to how the business is run, to control costs and improve profitability and/or cost effectiveness in non-profit organisations.

Here are some of the things that I've found using this method of recording and analysing employee hours. (None of these have been invented!)

- Large discrepancies between the price charged for a job and the actual time spent on it.
- A much clearer and accurate understanding of the distribution of employee hours spent on the various tasks and the individuals working on them.
- That some revenue streams were grossly unprofitable, requiring changes to them and in some cases simple abandonment.

- Some 80 per cent of the support activity being used on only 20 per cent of the customers from whom the revenue came. (The 80:20 ratio wasn't much of a surprise. Have a look at Pareto analysis if you're not already familiar with it.) More importantly I could identify which customers were in the 20 per cent and so could do something about it.

- That a more effective way of working could generate the same revenue with very much less employee time.

- There were overhead activities being carried out that were simply not needed at all, or that up to 90 per cent of the effort being expended on them could be saved.

Conclusion

It is essential to continuously run some type of recording and analysis of where employees' time is being used. It will take a bit of effort to set a system up and get it running smoothly, but it will repay dividends over and over again.

Activity based costing (ABC)

In the past few decades conventional methods of allocating overheads to product lines have been under close scrutiny, especially in the modern environments of multiple products, frequent introduction of new products, customisation of standard products, and higher ratios of overhead to direct costs.

This scrutiny focused initially on manufacturing where the difficulties encountered with conventional costing methods were perceived to be most significant. More recently, and with the development of new approaches to costing, attention has also turned to non-manufacturing industries.

Traditional costing methods

In the simplest case of a company selling a single product (Product A), all overheads can be regarded as production overheads and allocated to the product. So if overheads for the year are £1,000,000 and 75,000 items are produced annually then:

Overheads allocated to Product A	=	£1,000,000
Production overhead per unit @ 1,000,000 / 75,000	=	£13.33

If an additional product line (Product B) is introduced which has the same direct costs per item, is produced at a rate of 25,000 annually, and overheads increase to £1,200,000 p.a. and these are allocated to the product lines in direct proportion to their production volume then:

Overheads allocated to Product A	75,000 of 100,000 units = 75% = £900,000
Overheads allocated to Product B	25,000 of 100,000 units = 25% = £300,000
Total overheads 900,000 + 300,000	= £1,200,000
Overhead per unit A or B	£1,200,000 / 100,000 = **£12.00**

This approach relies upon the assumption that all overheads are used in direct proportion to product volume, and in most circumstances this will be the case, or as near to it as makes no appreciable difference. Also, if overheads are small in relation to direct costs, any error introduced by the use of volume proportional allocation will be correspondingly small.

brilliant disaster

If overheads are relatively high with respect to direct costs and there is a significant difference in the use of overheads for each product, then allocation of the overheads based only on product volumes will result in misrepresentation of the true cost of each product.

The principles of ABC

Continuing with the costs above, suppose that of the £1,200,000 overheads, £500,000 is spent on labour for machine maintenance, and that due to higher technology 60 per cent of the £500,000 is used for Product B, and 40 per cent for Product A. Clearly a more accurate representation of product costs will be obtained if account is taken of this difference.

For simplicity assume that the remaining 'Other' £700,000 of production overheads are correctly allocated proportionally to product volume. Then:

	Product A	**Product B**
Machine maintenance	£500,000 × 0.40 = £200,000	£500,000 × 0.60 = £300,000
'Other' overhead	£700,000 × 0.75 = £525,000	£700,000 × 0.25 = £175,000
Total overhead allocated	£725,000	£475,000
Overhead per unit	£725,000 / 75,000 = **£9.66**	£475,000 / 25,000 = **£19.00**

Compare the overhead cost per unit on page 282 with that above. If these represent a significant proportion of the total product costs, then it is clear that the difference should be taken into consideration for purposes such as product budgeting, cost control and selling price decisions.

Figures 12.1 and 12.2 illustrate this simple example.

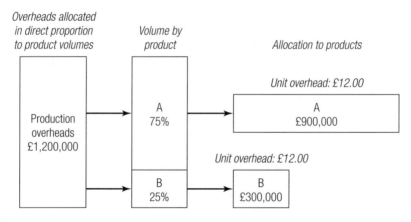

Figure 12.1 Conventional costing

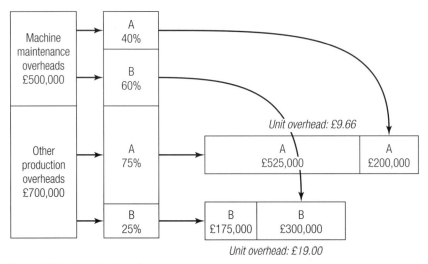

Figure 12.2 Activity based costing

These, in very simple terms, are the principles of (ABC). Whereas in conventional costing overheads are absorbed by product lines using only one or two commonly applied bases, such as output volume or direct labour hours, or number of orders, in the ABC illustration we use the *cost driver* activity of maintenance labour as the basis for the allocation of that particular overhead to product lines, and other overheads will similarly be allocated on the basis of the activities driving them.

In practice, ABC is usually applied to a wide and complex range of overheads from which activity based cost pools are created and cost driver rates derived: these are then applied to the appropriate product lines.

Summary

In this chapter we have:

- outlined a method for deciding which costs to start with;
- discussed the use of absolute figures and percentages;
- considered production purchases, consumption and cost from suppliers;
- looked in detail at the importance of measuring and controlling labour costs;
- viewed various methods for allocating, recording and analysing time spent;
- looked briefly at activity based costing.

PART 7

A practical forecasting framework

The illustration framework we have been using up to now is designed to enable you to understand the key aspects of budgeting and forecasting and, although it could be used in practice it's not laid out in the most convenient way. This part describes in detail a downloadable forecasting framework that you can use as the basis of your own system.

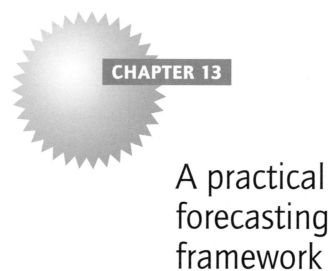

CHAPTER 13

A practical
forecasting
framework

This chapter is about ...

Introducing you to a practical forecasting monitoring template (included in the downloaded example pack as Practical Forecasting Template.xls) which is a useful starting point for your specific needs. It also includes a number of practical features that we've not yet covered.

Note: This chapter is intended for use with the downloaded version, and there are no step-by-step instructions for building it, although some elements are described in detail.

Features and uses of the practical template

The template is primarily designed for year-on-year forecasting and monitoring of financial performance, including:

- sales volumes
- sales unit prices
- revenue
- work in progress
- direct costs
- gross profit (of all revenue streams)
- salaries and related taxes
- a range of common overhead costs
- total operating costs
- depreciation
- operating profit before tax
- capital allowances
- corporation tax
- profit after tax
- shareholder dividends
- P&L account figures for the balance sheet
- retained profit (shareholder's funds)
- cash flow.

Structure of the practical template

The template consists of the following worksheets or tabs:

- sales and direct costs
- profit and loss/budget
- cash flow
- asset register with depreciation calculations.

Within the sections that follow, the blocks are addressed in the order, top to bottom, in which they appear.

⏎ brilliant reminder

The revenue and expense headings and groupings used in the forecast must exactly match the headings and groupings used in the book-keeping system or whatever method is used to record actual figures. If they don't, then updating the forecast with actual figures will be more difficult or even impossible.

There aren't any built-in sections for original forecast snapshots or for calculating variances – they aren't needed for the month end routine used later – but of course you can easily add them in if required.

Sales and direct costs

Here are the steps you will need.

Sales streams volume forecasts
- Enter sales streams – volumes.
- Enter sales streams – price per unit.
- Calculate sales streams revenues.

Direct costs
- Enter fixed/constant direct costs.
- Enter variable costs per item.
- Calculate variable costs.

Profit and loss/budget

Here are the steps you will need.

Sales revenue

- Additional actual and What if forecast. This has two uses, firstly a figure can be entered for forecasting additional monthly revenues in column R, then the actual figures for the month can overwrite the formulae as the year proceeds.

- Sales revenue is picked up from the Sales and Direct Costs worksheet.

- Other additional and *ad hoc* income can be entered, usually as actual figures as the year proceeds.

Work in progress (WIP)

- This row enables work in progress to be accounted for. As the heading WIP (invoice in advance)/work done implies, invoices that have been issued in advance of doing work can be entered as negative figures, then replaced as and when the work relating to the invoice is actually done.

  For example, in the downloaded template an amount of £2,500 has been entered as invoicing in advance, i.e. as a negative figure thus reducing the P&L revenue for the month by that amount. Then the work is shown as being done over the following three months with the appropriate amount of revenue being 'taken' until the original £2,500 has been used up, in this case as £1,250, then £750 then £500.

Actual sales revenue

The way in which this row is used will be described in the section on month end routines towards the end of this chapter.

Direct costs

- Calculated direct costs are picked up from the Sales and Direct Costs worksheet.

- Additional *ad hoc* direct costs can be entered each month as the year progresses.

Gross profit

- Calculated by subtracting the total direct costs from the total revenue.

Overheads

A range of typical overhead costs are included:

- Salaries – the gross salary paid to employees, i.e. if earning £30,000 p.a. enter 30,000 / 12 = £2,500.
- Bonuses – the gross bonus figure paid to employees.
- Employers' NIC – this is the National Insurance Contribution paid by employers on salaries and bonuses. The NIC percentage can be entered in column R.
- Sub-contactors/Temps – the costs for any workers not on the company payroll.
- Recruitment expenses.
- Training costs.
- Rent – all rental costs spread over the year.
- Insurance – all of the company's insurance spread over the year.
- Travel expenses.
- Sales and Marketing.
- Postage.
- Telephone – office.
- Telephone – mobile.
- IT Repairs and Consumables.
- Stationery.
- Internet Access.
- Website hosting.
- Legal fees.
- Accountancy fees.
- Other professional fees.
- Office machine maintenance.
- Premises.
- Bank charges.
- Charitable donations.
- Subscriptions.

- Refreshments.
- Miscellaneous overheads – use the miscellaneous heading with extreme caution, any figures put in here will be lost to useful analysis.
- Leasing.
- Contingency – not a must, but a strong recommendation to allow for the unforeseeable. The monthly amount depends on your business, but 5 per cent of total costs might be a good starting point.

Total operating costs

- Total operating costs are the sum of the overheads.

Total direct + Operating costs

- Direct costs plus the overheads.

Depreciation

- The amount charged to depreciation each month. Calculation of depreciation is done in the Asset Register, which we'll be looking at later. It's the annual figure that HMRC will need for tax calculations, and so if monthly figures are entered they must add up to the yearly figure, which of course will change if more capital purchases are made later in the business's financial year.

Operating profit before tax

- The operating profit before tax is the total revenue less the total direct and operating costs less depreciation. Before tax means before accounting for any corporation tax that might be due.

Tax and dividend

> **Warning**: The principles and factors used to calculate rows in this block are determined by legislation. Do not use any of them without checking the current regulations first.

- Capital allowance – some or all costs incurred on capital expenditure can be deducted from the profit assessed for corporation tax. The asset register worksheet that we'll look at later enables us to calculate the capital allowance.

- Add back depreciation – in this row the depreciation is added back, because depreciation unlike other expenses is not tax deductible. However, the allowance for capital expenditure has already been made in the row above.

- Corporation tax due on – calculated from 'Operating profit before tax' less the 'Capital allowance' plus 'Depreciation'.

- Corporation tax due – calculated by multiplying the 'Corporation tax due on' figure by the percentage in column R.

- Profit after tax – calculated by subtracting the 'Corporation tax due' from the 'Operating profit'.

Retained profit and P&L

- Retained profit brought forward – the retained profit brought forward from the previous year.

- Dividends – dividends paid to shareholders.

- P&L account after tax and dividends – the P&L account figure which, at the year end, will be in the balance sheet.

- Retained profit (Shareholder's funds) – carried forward to the next year.

Cumulative

- A block of useful cumulative figures. Add to them as required.

VAT calculations

Although VAT is a matter ultimately for the cash forecast, because this model is for VAT invoice accounting it's convenient to pick the figures up here in the P&L, where the invoice timing is available. The payment due to HMRC is picked up in the cash forecast.

- VAT rate – the VAT rate as a percentage.

- VAT due on sales – calculates the VAT due on all sales. If some revenue doesn't have VAT associated with it, such as bank interest, either separate it in the revenue block for the purpose of calculating VAT, or use the same principle applied to purchases below.

- VAT due on purchases – put 'V' in column A against all expenses liable to VAT. The VAT due is then calculated using, in column C for example,

```
=(SUMIF($A38:$A66,
"=V",C38:C66)+SUMIF($A30:$A32,
"=V",C30:C32))*$C96
```

which sums only those rows in each of overheads and direct costs that have 'V' in the corresponding row in column A, then multiplies by the VAT percentage rate.

- Net VAT due – calculated by subtracting 'VAT due on purchases' from 'VAT due on sales'.

- Quarterly payment due – calculated by adding the three months of each quarter.

Cash forecast

Cash in

- Cash in – from all sources. This can be broken down into more detail as required. The cash receipts are offset one month after the date of invoice. The figure for January in the template is a dummy picked up from the adjacent month.

Cash out

- Direct costs – are assumed to be paid in the same month as they are incurred.

- Net Salaries – are paid in the same month.

- Net Bonuses – are paid in the same month.

- PAYE – is paid in the month following. The figure for January in the template is a dummy picked up from the adjacent month.

- NI – is paid in the month following. The figure for January in the template is a dummy picked up from the adjacent month.

- Other overheads – all costs except those above are assumed to be paid in the same month they are incurred.

- VAT – is paid one month after the quarter end to which it relates.

- Corporation tax – no figure entered.

- Dividends – are paid in the same month.

Asset register

The asset register, apart from being a record of assets, provides calculations for:

- Months of depreciation to date and remaining for each item.

- Monthly depreciation per item and total.

- Cumulative depreciation per item and total.
- Net book value (NBV) per item and total.
- Capital allowance for the current year. (**Note:** The capital allowance principles and percentages depend upon current legislation, and so the examples in the template must not be regarded as being correct.)

Depreciation and net book value

Note: Set the month for which figures are required in cell D7. The month entered here displays in blue at the head of some of the columns.

The columns in the asset register are:

- **Reference** – simply a unique reference number. I recommend using the purchase order number for the item, which means it can easily be referred to for more detail and saves having that detail in the spreadsheet.
- **Item** – a short description of the item.
- **Serial number** – it can be useful to record any unique serial number on the item, either the manufacturer's or an in-house one.
- **Each** – the unit cost of the item, excluding VAT.
- **Qty** – the number of units bought.
- **Cost** – calculated cost of the purchase. (Each × Qty)
- **Acq Date** – the date of the purchase, i.e. the date on the purchase invoice. The column is formatted to display month and year, the day is not important.
- **Dep over mths** – the number of months over which the item is being depreciated. In this example all of the items are being depreciated over 36 months.
- **Months of dep until (month in blue)** – calculates the number of months since the purchase date to the date displayed in blue.
- **Mths left** – calculates the number of months of depreciation remaining, if any.

- **Mthly Dep** – calculates the monthly depreciation for each item.
- **Dep in (month in blue)** – calculates the depreciation, if any, for each item.
- **Cumulative Dep to (month in blue)** – calculates the cumulative depreciation for each item.
- **NBV (month in blue)** – calculates the Net Book Value of each item at the month in blue.

Capital allowance

brilliant disaster

The principle and percentages in this section were correct at the time of writing, but before live use check the current legislation or you could be in trouble!

- Enter the business's financial year end date in cell S5. The financial 'From' and 'To' dates below it are automatically calculated.
- Enter the capital allowance percentages – check current legislation – years 1, 2 and 3 as appropriate.
- The model calculates the allowance for each of years 1, 2 and 3 as appropriate and displays the annual total. The monthly figure to its right can be used for monthly accounts as required, but remember that the annual figure is the one used for HMRC tax calculations.

A typical month end routine

A 'typical' month end routine for recording actual figures and analysing them: perhaps typical isn't the right word, every organisation's month end routine will be different, but the reason for including it here is to provide a starting point and some ideas for creating your own.

The practical forecasting template as downloaded is shown as if the month end routine has been carried out at the end of month 2.

Objectives

A month end routine isn't essential, but is strongly recommended. The simple one described here will take an hour or so and will:

- provide a statement of profitability at the end of each month;
- update the forecast of profit and cash at the year end;
- enable a check on the accuracy of the forecast to date;
- highlight any upcoming problems with cash flow, enabling them to be anticipated and corrected while there is still time.

Of course the routine could be carried out at longer intervals, but the time it would take to do it every two months will be a lot more than double that for each month.

The routine

This simple routine could be a lot more complicated, especially if you want detailed historical analysis to be available, but it provides a solid and clear picture that is more than enough for most requirements.

The actual figures for the month could come from a variety of sources, depending upon how things are done in your business. I can't make too many assumptions about that, but I can and must assume that your book-keeping system is kept fully up to date at least monthly. If it isn't then a monthly routine on the forecasts can't be done.

The other important assumption, explained in Chapter 5, is that the headings and groups of headings used in the forecast match those used in the book-keeping system.

Entering actual figures in the P&L forecast

Note: No actual figures will be entered in the Sales and Direct Costs tab. In this way the original or updated forecast is always available to refer back to as required.

brilliant tip

I find it easiest to highlight forecast figures with a light colour at the outset, and remove the highlight when actual figures have been entered. In the template it shows that actual figures have been entered up to month 2. Except where explicitly stated there is no need to overwrite any formulae.

brilliant reminder

Remember that it's invoices for sales and expenses incurred that are required here, not the cash movements, although of course in some cases (e.g. salaries) they will be the same.

- **Sales revenue** – either insert actual figures into each of the sales rows overwriting the link formulae, or simply delete all of the links for the month you're working on and put a single sales figure in the 'Actual Sales Revenue' row.

- **Direct costs** – insert actual figures into each of the direct costs rows overwriting the link formulae.

- **Overheads** – insert actual figures into each of the overhead rows overwriting any forecast figures and formulae. By definition there will never be an actual figure for contingency – whatever the unexpected item was will be included under the appropriate direct cost or overhead heading.

- **Depreciation** – enter the monthly deprecation figure from the asset register overwriting any forecast figure.

- **Capital allowance (Tax and dividend block)** – if you wish, enter a monthly figure *as a minus quantity* from the asset register. Or, you can simply update the year figure and leave the individual months blank. If you do put monthly figures in they will need to be adjusted later if new capital purchases are made, which will of course affect the annual allowance. In any event the total of the capital allowance for the year must be the same as indicated in the asset register.

- **Dividends** – enter the total of any dividends that have been declared for the month or period ending in the month.

Entering actual figures in the cash forecast

There are several options for dealing with the cash forecast.

- For example, you can overwrite each of the forecast values for 'Cash In' and 'Cash Out', in which case the bank figures will be calculated in the usual way.

- Alternatively, a history of cash transactions in and out may not be of any real use, so simply overwrite the closing balance of the month you are dealing with and either leave or delete the formulae for 'Cash In' and 'Cash Out'. This is what I would do and what has been done in the template at the end of month 2.

Review after entering the actual figures

Having entered the actual figures spend a few minutes looking over them and, as appropriate, comparing with the forecast. For example, ask yourself the following questions:

- In the light of the sales year to date does the forecast for the rest of the year need to be adjusted?

- If the sales forecast is adjusted, are there any constant direct costs or variable directs that aren't linked to the sales volumes that need to be adjusted?

- Consider the overhead expenditure. For any significant costs is the monthly forecast in line with the average year to date?

- How is the 'P&L account after tax and dividends' for the year end looking? Does any action need to be taken in good time if all is not as you'd like it to be?

- Has the forecast amount of corporation tax altered much since last month? Do you need to make a change to the provision for it that you have allowed in next year's cash forecast?

- How is the cash forecast looking, and are there any danger spots ahead? Is there a shortfall forecast that it would be best to speak to the bank about sooner rather than later?

⏎ brilliant reminder

Your business is unique. These review points are just examples, so look for any others that are more relevant to you.

Summary

In this chapter we have:

- described a practical forecasting framework that can be used as a basis for your own system;
- considered its features and uses, together with the detail of its structure;
- followed a 'typical' month end routine for entering actual figures in the P&L and cash forecasts.

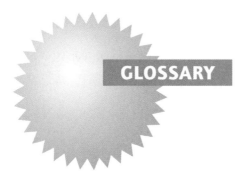

GLOSSARY

This glossary covers the principal budget and forecasting terms used in the book.

Activity based costing (ABC) A method of allocating overhead costs across product/service lines.

Asset An item of realisable value.

Asset register A record of the purchase price and depreciation of items of realisable value.

Budget Used by itself the term usually refers to *budget allocation*.

Budget allocation Financial limits allocated to *expense* and *revenue* headings, often calendarised.

Budget forecast Expected *revenue* and *expenses* for a budgeting period, based on rational considerations and experience.

Capital expenditure (expense/cost) Expenditure on items that possess a realisable value. See also *asset*.

Cash in The cash received for *revenue* earned. Also known as *income*.

Cash out The cash paid out for *costs* (or expenses) incurred.

Constant direct cost Costs associated directly with the product, but not significantly affected by product volumes.

Cost Incurred *expense*, not necessarily yet paid for by *cash out*.

Credit (days/weeks, etc.) In forecasting, the period of time between *cost* and *cash out*, or between *revenue* and *cash in*.

Creditor The one to whom money is owed. See also *debtor*.

Debtor The one from whom money is due. See also *creditor*.

Depreciation The amount by which the value of a *fixed asset* reduces.

Direct cost Any cost directly associated with the product. See also *constant direct* and *variable direct* cost.

Expense (expenditure/cost) See *cost*.

Fixed asset An item of realisable value.

Gross profit Profit after *direct costs* are deducted from the *revenue*.

Income See *cash in*.

Indirect (cost) Another word for *overheads*.

Loss A negative value of *profit*.

Net profit Profit after *overheads* are deducted from *gross profit*.

Overhead (cost) Costs not directly associated with a product.

Period The time interval between successive forecasting elements – usually one calendar month or four weeks.

Profit A loose term, most often used instead of *net profit*.

Revenue The value of *income* earned, but not necessarily received. See *cash in*.

Span The time span of a budget (or other) forecast. Usually one year.

Variable direct cost Costs directly associated with the product, and which vary significantly according to product volumes.

'What if' A general term for the testing of possible circumstances, strategic proposals and the like.

Index

absolute addresses in Excel 47–8
  copying 48
activity-based budgets (ABB) 102
activity-based costing (ABC) 272,
    281–4
  principles 282–4
  and traditional methods 281–2
addressing, relative in Excel 47–8
arrow keys in Excel 60
asset register 295–7
assets 150
automatic recalculation in
    spreadsheets 71–2
averages in Excel 92–3

backing up work in spreadsheets 67
budget 5, 6, 104
  assembling 145–67
  in central supporting role 6
  charts and key indicators 160–7
  in operational role 7
budget allocation 6, 7, 105, 209–10
budget calculations for VAT 258–60
budget control 105
  delegation of 107
budget forecast 5, 6, 7
  adjustment and refinement 171–2
  example 81–5
  in example budget 127–31
  making 150–8
  setting up monitoring of 219–22
  see also causes and effects
budget management 25–6
budgeting methods 100–3

budgeting process in example budget
  budget forecast 127–31
  cash flow forecast 131–40
  cost categories 108–18
    capital 109–10, 118
    constant direct costs 112–13
    overheads 113–14
    start up 110–11
    variable direct costs 111–12
  cost headings 114–18
  forecast's duration and period 121
  requirements of 106
  revenue headings 120
  review of 104
  sales forecast 125–6
  single or departmental 107–8

capital
  and cash flow 175–6
  in cost headings 118
  in example budget 109–10
capital allowance, month end routine
    for 299
capital costs 150–1
capital expenditure, causes and effects
    175–6
cash accounting for VAT 256, 264
cash flow 9
  changes, impact of 241–7
    flat sales profile 242
    sales volume peaks 243–4
    smooth sales growth 244–5
    and timing 246–7
  forecast 29–30, 86–9, 104

cash flow (*Continued*)
  importance of 10–11
  rapid growth of 248–9
    and bank loans 249
  reviewing 233–5
  sales volume
    effect of 245–6
    peaks in 243–4
cash flow control 30, 104
cash flow forecast adjustments 158–60
cash flow forecast
  adjustment and refinement 171–2
  in example budget 131–40
    creating 133–40
  forecasting template for 295
  setting up monitoring of 222–3
  and VAT calculations 261–4
  see also causes and effects
cash in 9, 243, 295
cash out 9, 243, 295
causes and effects
  addressing both 180–1
  cause known, what effect 191–8
    capital 193
    constant direct costs, increased
      194–5
    overheads costs 191–2
    single large expense 193
    start up 193
    timing changes 195–7
  cost factors 175–8
    capital expenditure 175–6
    constant direct costs 177–8
    overheads 178
    start up expenditure 176–7
    variable direct costs 177
  effect known, causes needed 181–90
    gross profit, improving 181–6
    trial and error on 187–90
  examining 173
  and gross profitability 199–201
  sales factors 174–5
    sales prices 175
    sales volumes 174–5

simple cause and effect 173–80
  summary 179–80
  timing factors 178–9
    cash payment timing 178
    sales receipt timing 179
cell contents, copying in Excel 42–3
cell notes in Excel 60
cell protection in spreadsheets 69
charts 160–1, 164–5
charts and graphs in Excel 55
check sum in spreadsheets 70–1
clarity of forecasts 205, 206–7
closing balances and VAT 263
columns in Excel
  fixed headings 89–91
  inserting and deleting 49–51
  width of 42
constant direct costs
  causes and effects 177–8
    increase in 194–5
  in cost headings 119
  in example budget 112–13
  and gross profit 182
  measuring 275
    allocating time spent 277–8
    analysis 280–1
    manpower costs 275
    recording time spent 279–80
  reviewing 231
cost cash flow forecast 86–7
cost categories in example budget
      108–18
  capital 109–10
  constant direct costs 112–13
  overheads 113–14
  start up 110–11
  variable direct costs 111–12
cost control 27–8
cost factors, causes and effects 175–8
  capital expenditure 175–6
  constant direct costs 177–8
  overheads 178
  start up expenditure 176–7
  variable direct costs 177

cost headings in example budget
    114–18
  categorising 118–20
  choosing 117–18
costs 108
  measuring and controlling 271–2
    absolute figures and percentages
    272
  manpower costs 275–81
  from production 274–5
  purchases 273–4
  from suppliers 274
  which costs 272
Ctrl key in Excel 59–60
cumulative totals in Excel 93–4
cursor, moving in spreadsheets 40–1

database functions 44
date and time functions 44
de Bono, Edward 206
debtor days 248
deleting rows and columns 49–51
depreciation 8
  in example budget 109
  forecasting template for 293, 296–7
  month end routine for 299
direct costs 8
  forecasting template for 290, 291
  measuring and controlling 271–2
  month end routine for 299
  variable and constant 182
dividends, forecasting template for
    293–4, 299
duration of forecast in example budget

Excel
  arrow keys 60
  averages in 92–3
  cell notes 60
  Ctrl key 59–60
  cumulative totals in 93–4
  fixed column and row headings
    89–91

freeze panes 90–1
linking 83
paste special 60–1
percentages in 91–2
principal facilities and functions
    40–58
  absolute addresses 47–8
  cell contents, copying 42–3
  charts and graphs 55
  column width 42
  formatting 51–5
  functions 43–6
  justification 52
  naming ranges 57–8
  numbers, entering 41
  ranges 56
  text, entering 41
  relative addressing 47–8
  split Window 89–90
  toolbars 58–9
  totals 59
expenditure 150
expense accrual 235–6

file linking 83
finance, raising 28–30
financial functions 44
fixed assets 109
fixed budgets 102–3
fixed period forecasts 18
flat sales profile 242
flexible budgets 103
forecasting template 289–300
  asset register 295–7
  cash forecast 295
  features and uses of 289
  month end routine 297–300
    objectives 298
    review 300
    steps 298–300
  profit/loss budget 291–5
  sales and direct costs 290
  structure of 290

forecasts
  adjustment and refinement 171–2
  clarity 205, 206–7
  correctness 20–2
  delegation of 107
  in example budget
    duration and period 121
  examples 72–89
    budget forecast 81–5
    cash flow forecast 86–9
    sales forecast 72–81
  objectives of 99–100
  relevance 205, 207–8
  reviewing 226–36
  visibility 205, 206
formatting in Excel 51–5
freeze panes in Excel 90–1
functions in Excel 43–6
  copying 46–7

gross profit 112
  causes and effects 179
  and direct costs 181, 182
  forecasting template for 292
  and sales, ratio 182
gut feelings 27

incremental budgets 101
information functions 44
inserting rows and columns 49–51
invoice accounting for VAT 256,
  257–60

justification in Excel 52

key figure copy of operational budget
  213, 216
key indicators 160–4
key ratios 165–7

linking in Excel 83
logical functions 44
long-term planning cycles 16–17
lookup and reference functions 44
loss 8

manpower costs, measuring 275–81
math and trig functions 44
medium-term planning cycles 17
minimum balance indicator 161
monitoring of operational budgets
  principles 210–17
    actual figures 211
    comparison of actual figures
      212–16
    frequency 210
    invoice or payments 211–12
  recording actual figures 224–6
  reviewing 226–36
  setting up 217–24
    budget forecast 219–22
    cash flow forecast 222–3
    sales forecast 217–18
  variances 229–30
monitoring of VAT calculations 264
multiple worksheet linking 83

net profit 8
  causes and effects 179
  and revenue 181
nominal codes 115–16
nominal ledger 115–16
numbers, entering in Excel 41

operational budgets 209–10
  performance monitoring principles
    210–17
    actual figures 211
    comparison of actual figures
      212–16
    frequency 210
    invoice or payments 211–12
  reviewing 226–36
overheads costs 8
  activity-based costing on 281–4
  and cash flow 192
  causes and effects 178
  in cost headings 119–20
  in example budget 113–14
  forecasting template for 292–3

measuring manpower costs 275
month end routine for 299
and net profit 191–2
reviewing 231

paper budget copy of operational
   budget 213, 214, 216
paste special in Excel 60–1
payment of VAT 256–7
percentages in Excel 91–2
period of forecast in example budget
   121
perpetual forecasts 19–20
planning, and 'what if' 26–7
planning cycles 15–17
production, measuring costs from
   274–5
   purchase costs 274
profit 8
profit and loss forecast 8
   forecasting template for 291–5
      depreciation 293
      direct costs 291
      gross profit 292
      overheads 291–2
      retained profit 294
      sales revenue 291
      tax and dividend 293–4, 299
      total operating costs 293
      VAT 294–5
      work in progress 291
   month end routine for 298–9
profitability 29
   causes and effects on 199–201
   reviewing 231–2
purchase repayment 236
purchases costs, measuring 273–4
   production costs 274

ranges in Excel 56
   naming 57–8
reiteration process 172
relative addressing in Excel 47–8

relevance of forecasts 205, 207–8
revenue headings in example budget
   120
reviewing VAT calculations 264
rolling forecasts 19
rows in Excel, inserting and deleting
   49–51

salary costs, measuring 276
sales accrual 235–6
sales factors, causes and effects 174–5
   sales prices 175
   sales volumes 174–5
sales forecast
   adjustment and refinement 171–2
   example 72–81
   in example budget 125–6
   forecasting template for 290
   making 147–9
   month end routine for 299
   setting up monitoring of 217–18
   see also causes and effects
sales growth, smooth 244–5
sales profile, flat 242
sales repayment 236
sales volume
   cash flow, effect on 245–6
   peaks in 243–4
same worksheet linking 83
saving work in spreadsheets 66–7
short-term planning cycles 17
single large expense and cash flow 193
smooth sales growth 244–5
span of forecast 121
split Window in Excel 89–90
spreadsheet copies of operational
   budget 213, 214–16
spreadsheets 38–9
   cursor, moving around 40–1
   essential practices and conventions
      65–72
      automatic recalculation 71–2
      backing up 67

spreadsheets (*continued*)
    cell protection 69
    check sum 70–1
    date and time stamping 68
    saving work 66–7
    version numbers 68
    example forecasts 72–89
        budget forecast 81–5
        cash flow forecast 86–9
        sales forecast 72–81
    size 40
    see also Excel
start up costs in example budget
    110–11
    in cost headings 118
start up expenditure and cash flow
    176–7
statistical functions 44
SUM function 45
suppliers, measuring costs from 274

taxation, forecasting template for
    293–4, 299
text in Excel
    entering 41
    functions 44
timing factors, causes and effects
    178–9
    cash payment timing 178
    sales receipt timing 179
toolbars in Excel 58–9
totals in Excel 59

variable direct costs
    causes and effects 177
    in cost headings 119
    in example budget 111–12
    and gross profit 182
    measuring 275
    per item 151–4
    reviewing 231
    savings on 184
variances in operational budgets
    229–30
VAT 255–65
    budget calculations 258–60
    calculations 257–60
    cash accounting for 256, 264
    and cash flow forecast 261–4
    and closing balances 263
    definition 255–6
    in example budget 132
    forecasting template for 294–5
    invoice accounting for 256, 257–60
    monitoring and reviewing 264
    payment of 256–7
    see also taxation
version numbers in spreadsheets 68
visibility of forecasts 205, 206

'what if' analysis
    and budget forecasts 249–50
    in planning 26–7

zero based budgets (ZBB) 102